Racism:
The Absence of Good

DR. CHRISTOPHER D. HANDY, PHD

By: Dr. Christopher D. Handy, PhD

Dedication

This book is dedicated to my Lord and Savior Jesus Christ, who saved me and changed me into the person I am today and for His saving Grace, I am forever grateful.

I dedicate this book to Mankind and to all of the people who have suffered, struggled and died at the hands of those who practice racism and discrimination.

To all of my brothers and sisters who strive daily to eradicate the scars of racism by bringing an end to this evil that has plague our society for far too long. I applaud those courageous individuals who stand in the gap amid adversity promoting unity, brotherhood, and love among all people, while standing for justice.

Acknowledgement

I like to acknowledge my Lord and Savior Jesus Christ, for without His wisdom and insight this book would have not been possible.

I applaud those courageous men and women who stand in the gap daily promoting unity and brotherhood among all people, and who stand for justice and who strives daily working to bring peace and real change to our world by educating and combating the effects of racism.

I wish to personally acknowledge The 44th President of The United States of America, The Honorable Barack H. Obama. Mr. President, I applaud your strong, dedicated, and courageous leadership that has propelled this nation forward. Your Presidency has open doors that can never be close and close doors that will never be open ever again, for that I am forever thankful. You are truly an inspiration and a real American Hero, thank you for all that you have done and will do to help make this nation and the world a better place for all of humanity, may God richly bless and keep you.

I acknowledge my lovely family, my lovely children, Kendrick, Kendra, Adia, Lavelle, Christopher Rachelle, and Casey, and my adorable grandchildren. I acknowledge my Mother Georgia Mae Handy, my three sisters Caroline Handy, Patricia Johnson, Pamela Slack and my Brother-in-laws, nieces, nephews, my uncles (Leroy Handy and Roosevelt (Duck) Handy, aunts, and cousins

I acknowledge all of my good and dear friends who stood by me and encouraged me throughout this project. My mentor and friend Dr. Charles G. Adams, Senior Pastor of the Hartford Memorial Baptist Church in Detroit, Michigan and Church family. Mr. John Shamblin, his lovely wife Jennifer and their family. Rev. Lynn Malone Pastor of First United Methodist Church in Monroe, LA and family. Bishop Bradley Carey and his Lovely wife Amy, Bishop John Thomas and his family, Attorney Zebe Grayson and family, Mr. Roy N. Shelling and his lovely wife Brenda and family, Dr. Monica Handy Publisher, Editor, Owner of Coming Out Of The Wilderness Magazine (COOTW) and family, Dr.

Jacqueline L. Olson and family, Dr. Karen Stubblefield and family, Dr. Richard L. Hoffman, Jr. and family, and Dr. Katie Honeycutt and family.

Lastly but not forgotten, those who have gone on to be with the Lord. In remembrance of my Grand Father and Grand Mother Mr. and Mrs. George and Lillie Mae Handy, My Dad Louis Potter, My Uncle Jimmy Handy, My Grand Mother Rosetta Potter, and my friend Al Holiday, and my Professor and good dear friend Dr. Virgil Vanderburg.

Foreword

It is important to understand the nature of racism and intolerance. Racism is based on ignorance, stereotyping and learned hatred. Many people accept the fact that we live in a diverse society today and we need to appreciate different cultures. Although racism has been conditioned by economic essentials, but felt through the arts, media, and religion. However, there are still large segments of society that won't accept people of different races, cultures, religion, creed, or sex or that we need to work together in peace, love, unity and true brotherhood and sisterhood, if we are to survive as the human race.

The moral question facing us today, has anything good come out of the legacy of racism in this country? The answer is NO. Racism, regardless of where it comes from, or who it's against is wrong. There is no good in hating your brother or causing them unjust pain or destruction. Racism discriminates it leaves scars, brokenness, disharmony, and it kills. If we are to survive as human beings and become a community, then we need to make immediate changes within ourselves beginning with our attitudes in order to change our world as a whole.

Believe it or not, racism is a learned behavior. Just observe little children as they interact among themselves before they are fed the "negatives" of the differences between the races by their parents or guardians. For it was Jesus, the Son of God, who said that before we can enter into the Kingdom of Heaven, we must be like little children, that simply means being humble, friendly, quick to reconcile, loving, forgiving and caring.

There is no lack of evidence that racism persists. The attitude of racists is ridiculous and barbarous. We must strive daily to put an end to racism by any means necessary. This will only happen when everyone becomes humble and sensitive, when despair and craziness will not characterize our civilization, and when everyone succeeds in removing poisonous and negative influences from their conscience. Only then will compassion and wisdom eliminate absurdity and cruelty in its entirety.

Racism is an example of man's inhumanity to his fellowman. From this one belief system, numerous atrocities have been committed by man. Racism has barred Jews from their work and forced them out from their homes. They have flogged and whipped against the bleeding and stinging backs of Africans whose life has been characterized by sweat and toil. Native Americans have been forced on reservations after having their lands stolen from them with false treaties and broken promises which were never meant to be honored by the government. Of every immigrant to the United States, they have heaped coals of fire upon their backs. They incapacitated Asians who attempted to mine gold. With a smiling face they have imprisoned the innocent, lynched and burned people alive, thrown them out into the streets, beaten them and mutilated them. Through the means of hate and scorn racists individuals have committed countless of unspeakable horrors against humanity that was once thought only to happen in nightmares.

There are those who believe that because someone of a certain race committed a particular crime, hence the entire race has the tendency to commit the same crime. This however, is an incorrect reasoning and heavily flawed. The action of an individual can only represents the character and moral of that person. An individual race is not a moral agent, just as a government is not or a society is not. Every single individual is their own moral agent. Therefore, to hold red-haired people, green-eyed people, or dark skinned people responsible for the behavior of a few individuals is ridiculous.

Racism transcends beyond discrimination based on ethnicity or race alone. There also the insecurity and fear of losing the dominance or economic control which fuels the minds of people who promote racism.

Any society that accepts the philosophy of racism, whether covertly or overtly attracts a strong negative spirit of hate, hostility, dislike, bigotry and division among its people of different ethnicity or races. On the surface, such a society remains as one, but beneath it lie many pockets of division caused by racial prejudice.

United we stand and divided we fall. This basic sentence speaks volumes concerning the relevance of unity and its importance. Wherever there is unity, there is power and resilience to produce a peaceful existence among all people in a world that's has been plague with racial tension and division.

There is an urgent need for mankind to become a community and began working towards the common good of all mankind instead of trying to destroy one another. Until we can become a community that can live in peace and expresses love and unity towards one another, we will otherwise destroy ourselves. We must put aside our hatred for one another and look deep within ourselves and step outside of our comfort zone and reach out to others that are different from us. Only then can we begin to change our world and begin the process of bringing an end to racism once and for all and all of humanity can strive to live in peace, harmony, unity and love.

Lastly, let us unite and find a healthy solution to ending racism, it must begin with us and it must begin now. If we desire to see real change in our world, then the change must come from within each of us. Now the time has come for real change, let us begin.

Introduction

Racism: The Absence of Good is a book written to outline the many aspects of racism and how it has had a significant impact both on the individuals who experience it and those who encourage it. In this book we will examine the emotional effects racism has had on our society and world as a whole and how this plays a central role in our lives and in the lives of those around us.

Racism is a ideology that gives expression to the myths about other racial and ethnic groups, that devalues and renders inferior those groups, that reflects and is perpetuated by deeply rooted historical, social, cultural, and power inequalities in society. Racism is the result of a complex interplay of individual attitudes, social values and institutional practices. It is expressed in the actions of individuals and institutions and is promoted in the ideology of popular culture. It changes its form in response to social change. Racism has its roots in the belief that some people are superior because they belong to a particular race, ethnic or national group. This theory is a social construct, not a scientific one.

Racism like any other evil which comes only to steal, to kill and to destroy our human soul. It hunts down, possesses and haunts its perpetrators, human targets or wounded souls. Only a willing and receptive human soul can become recruits of a racist spirit. The door to your hearth as to be open before you can receive a mindset of the tradition of racism. Perhaps for some, accepting and perpetrating racism has its benefits within the society, especially in environments where economic dominance favors a racist culture. In other words, some Individuals feel like they need to support a system, whether it is fair or unfair that favors them economically. For humans there is always the driver by social adaptation for self-preservation. Therefore, racism within any society goes beyond just discrimination based on race or ethnicity. There is also the fear and insecurity of losing the economic control or dominance that fuels the minds of those who foster racism.

In this book it will show that racial hatred, violence, and discrimination significantly mediate the relationship between conscious commitments and practice, which has led to the absence of good in our society and in the world. Hence any society that accepts racism, whether overtly or covertly, invites in a very powerful negative spirit of dislike, hostility, hate, and separation as well as continuous division among its people of different races or ethnicity. Such a society remains on the surface as one, but underneath it has numerous pockets of division fueled by racial prejudice. As Christians or even non-Christians, there are positive steps which we as individuals can take to over come the spirit of racism.

What if we each tackle this fight in a way that can make a difference? What if instead of accepting it and enduring it as Dr. Martin Luther King Jr. so wisely stated "in appalling silence," if we each took a stand and spoke out against racial issues. What if we each began to insert it in to the threads of everyday conversation and when our conversations about racism hit the brick wall, instead of turning away from it as we always have, we instead continue our conversations about racism until they actually climb over the wall and become engaged in the same dialogue until they too began to discuss racial issues with one another. If we do this, we would be making a difference in the world. We would be setting an action in motion that perhaps will begin to take an life of its own and make its mark on the world.

This is why this book was written to tackle racism first hand and offer workable solutions to the problem facing our world today, enhance bringing about means to combat it and finding ways to work together. Racism can be vanquished now, where as future generations will be able to live in peace, unity, harmony and love. There is hope for our world and it can began now, with us building a bright new world and a better future.

Table of Contents

Chapter 1

What is Racism?

Racism is an abstract term: it is not an object which we can be held and observed closely. What can be seen is the effect which it produces. Perhaps it's a natural impulse which is common to all human beings to turn to the physical environment or outside world when confronted with a challenge that needs to be addressed or fixed.

Racism leads no place but to a dark abyss of lies, bigotry, deception, pain and suffering, division, hopelessness, inequality, intolerance, murder, and contempt of humanity. Racism is ugly. It divides people into "them" and "us", based upon a person skin color.

Racism is complicated, and the individual aspect of prejudice is well pronounced. But even worse is the fact that generations of racist attitudes are strongly woven into our systems and institutions in a poisonous way, hurting every one of us.

Therefore, we need to have a better understanding of what racism really is: its nature and sources and also unearth the beliefs and ideas that support this barbaric act and expose them so they are unable to give strength to racial discrimination any more.

Racism can be said to have originated from the inception of the slave trade in the western world. However, the genesis of this atrocity dates back centuries. Its inception lies in the hearts of men and the unfair judgment placed on the color of skin. Racism started from our ideas about what's right and wrong, and our ability to relate this with the concept of good and evil, and light and darkness.

Racism is an evil of a very high degree and it is evident through observation. In our society, being tagged a racist is among the greatest assault on one's character. And the word 'racism' itself has become so divisive, hostile and shameful that the topic is mostly avoided or downplayed in almost any discussion or debate except when intended to attack the character of someone or an opponent.

Racism is the most difficult challenge defying America. A country whose family line incorporates each individual on earth, whose standards of flexibility under law have motivated millions all through the world, can't keep on harboring preference against any racial or ethnic gathering without deceiving itself. Racism is an attack against human respect, a reason for disdain and division, a malady that demolishes society destroying peace, advancement and solidarity.

For instance a government can formulate policies, build infrastructure and create social programs as was the case in the late 50's in a bid to make amends for hundreds of years of unjust and cruel treatment meted out to an entire race. Although there is a place for this sort of reconciliation, it has little effect on the root problem which gave rise to racism and continues to act as a thorn in the flesh of our daily lives.

Despite efforts aimed at its elimination, racism keeps on working its abhorrence upon this country. Progress toward tolerance, harmony, mutual respect and solidarity has been agonizingly slow and mostly impeded with repeated setbacks. The late resurgence of divisive racial attitudes, increased racial incidents, and the deepening despair of perceived minorities and the poor requires urgent solutions. To ignore this problem any longer is to open this nation to more physical, moral and spiritual danger.

Bear in mind that victims of any protracted racial discrimination, mostly seek relief in the thought that Black Americans, White Americans, Native Americans, Hispanic Americans, Asian Americans, and Middle Eastern Americans are so unmistakably not the same as each other hence; every one of them must map out their social and cultural boundaries and stay within them. This is not sensible! It is a retreat from the truth of our common humanity and is bringing about further setbacks to our common advancement.

With situations of discrimination, people tend to associate towards groups of people similar to themselves; this is only natural and physical. Socioeconomic status also plays a part, as much as biological characteristics within and outside a given race. The overall effect is: to alienate, to inspire violence, to deny opportunities common to all and in most prevalent cases, to advance opportunities for the sake of gaining favor, making a name or acclaim benefits.

Meanwhile, like most concepts and ideas, racism has advanced with the times and is currently more camouflaged and harder to perceive. A few individuals may say that racism does not exist anymore or they can't spot it around them. Mainly because they wear blinders or don't want to see it for themselves or admit that racism exists. Well the fact of the matter is, we don't yet live in a post-racial world as racism still exists in everyone's psyche, as well as in the exceptionally social fabric of America.

However, change and continuous progress can only happen in our nation when individuals have the mindset that everybody is a human being and an American. Our leaders must come together to bring us all together for development, solidarity and peace that will improve life for all people. Our country is going downhill and people should look at getting her back on her feet, rather than looking at how to divide us through culture and heritage.

We must stop looking at the differences in our race, color and background, and begin talking and working together on how we need each other to build our country for the overall future of all our people and the world. Poor people are basically of every race. People are hungry and homeless, taxes and basic health cost are rising; people are losing their hopes. These and many other problems can only be solved by uniting all people to respect and make lasting changes together. Our country is in great need of all people to get beyond how we look and become the nation of solutions known to the world.

II.
A Proactive Approach:

Racism is not just the most important and persistent social problem in the world today, it is a cankerworm that has eaten deep into the different social systems of the world. And to even imagine that it is on the rise in increasing ways, calls for a more committed and proactive approach to putting it to an end. Racism has reeked so much havoc, and if nothing is done fast, the destructive effects would be too much to handle for future generations.

Racism is based on the belief that abilities and characteristics can be attributed to certain people on the basis of race, with the conception that some racial groups are superior to others. Racism and bigotry have been used as powerful tools to promote fear or even hatred of others in times of conflict and war, and also during economic downturns.

How then do we save the world from this social evil that is hell-bent on consuming even the generations unborn? This destructive effects can be nip in the bud only if we try.

Racism has been a very touchy subject for some groups of people, as issues hovering around free speech and Article 19 of the Universal Declaration of Human Rights[1] come into play. Some schools of thought argue that racial discrimination and prejudice are ordinary words and on the basis of free speech such views should be allowed to be aired without any form of restriction. Others hold the view that these words can lead to very serious and dire consequences.

At the heart of racism lie two important concepts: Ignorance and fear. All of us tend to have racial attitudes towards other people. This is usually

---

[1] Article 19 of the Universal Declaration of Human Rights http://www.ichrp.org

based on ignorance. All humans are prone to prejudge others based on limited knowledge, most especially if they are different from us. Most of what is considered as racial behavior in the society is due to ignorance of other groups and their social condition and way of life. Based on the way American society is structured, most white Americans have no basic knowledge or idea of life in the African American or Latino communities. This is simply because the norms of separation and segregation which prevent people from different racial/ethnic groups to interact fuels this so called ignorance of groups, which then gives rise to racial attitudes.

If any progress is to be achieved, then it would be worthwhile to suspend all prejudgments until all evidence is in.

III.

Building Bridges:

What can we do to save and preserve humanity from this evil? Saving and preserving humanity from this evil is only possible if all hands can be on deck and great commitment shown towards achieving something meaningful.

What are the practical steps the world can take in order to adjust it position along this spectrum? This is a crucial question, because, without it, all that has been said would be merely theory. From what has been said earlier, we have established that ignorance plays a critical role in fueling racism, and if anything worthwhile is to be achieved, the world must understand that there has to be a transition away from this current behavioral norm. This can only take place when we challenge the uncomfortable status quo we find ourselves in because of the belief in a higher principle.

Simply say there is an urgent need to socialize and also spend quality time together to build bridges of understanding, which by every mean eliminates those invisible walls that often times stand between us. Humanity always wants freedom and freedom from racial prejudice must be cultivated deliberately; the reason is because it goes against our natural tendency.

Now I offer this hard saying, just as the bible calls it in St. John 6:60: that we as Americans cannot claim that we have freed ourselves from racial prejudice until our living room is fully integrated. The question here is whether our social life reflects our values, and by what measure can we claim that we do not hold racial prejudice if our social life reflects these values?

Furthermore, the human race can authoritatively save itself from this social ill when white America take up the primary responsibility for bringing about equality; when this is accomplished, there will be no need for them to struggle for their own rights.

With all that has been proposed as regards to saving the world from the clutches of racism, one can only say it will become a thing of the past if those perpetrating this crime against humanity understand that it has led to unfathomable sufferings and massive death toll, and can view this social evil from a fresh perspective that is absent of any form of bias whatsoever. It is our task and our responsibility to resolve these racial issues now at this present moment and not leave them for future generations, it's up to us and we must work the work while time permits.

Together and united as a nation, there can be so much accomplished and so many solutions resolved to the many problems facing us by racism and prejudice. Together and united, all people working together can preserve the future of our nation and position it as the light to the entire world.

Chapter 2

No One Is Born A Racist

Racism is a difficult subject to tackle and in order to form a culture free of racism, we must begin with education. The premise of racism is based on ignorance, stereotyping and learned hatred. If you don't want your children to grow up in a world of hatred, teach them tolerance toward race, religion, color, and sexual orientation. We must expose racism and bigotry for what they are, a plague on society.

Racism is not an issue that will be easily resolved, and the sooner that we begin to work together the sooner we'll come to a solution. The question that lies before us, how does a society right the wrong of racism? Can it be done?

However, no one can change history or wipe out the evils of what has been committed in the past. But there is an legacy of racism that still persists today. It's invisible in many respects, yet it is like a energy that invades an room after an argument. Everyone can feel the tension to one degree or another, each reacting to it in one's own individual way, shaping his or her behavior consciously and unconsciously. Racism is not an object that one can hold in their hands and observe. We can only see the effects of what it produces.

This is why no one is born a racist, it is something that is taught, learned, and accepted as a way of life.

Racism is a learned behavior. If you don't believe it, just observe little children and the way they interact before being taught by parents and others the differences between the races. For it was Jesus, the Son of God, who said in St. Matthew 18:3 "Verily I say unto you, Except ye be converted, and become as little children, ye shall not enter into the Kingdom of Heaven."

It is in our characteristics as a society that there will be individuals in our general public who are distinctive. Tragically, there are likewise those in our middle who will humiliate and malign pretty much any abused individual or minority; Blacks, Whites, Native Americans, Hispanics, Jews, and even the destitute.

Parents, guardians, caregivers, and relatives should in this manner educate their children to acknowledge the different qualities in individuals with the goal that they will grow up free of prejudice and bias on the grounds that it is reasonable, as well as on the grounds that their lifestyle will rely upon it.

Nobody is conceived preferential. Around a child's second birthday, they naturally begin to perceive the differences and similarities between and around them. A little while later, their concept of what is great or fun gets to be impacted basically by the people around them – parents, guardians, caregivers, relatives, different adolescents and teachers.

Interestingly, prejudice punishes the child who is hated, as well as the one who hates. Children who are the target of prejudice habitually grow low self-esteem, and develop sentiments of hatred and outrage. They may attempt to support their own values by discovering a gathering or sect of people whom they can work with. On the other hand, children harboring bias create perplexity, misguided thinking, questions and blame. These traits provide a weak foundation for the development of a healthy self-esteem.

To start with, parents should recognize and subdue their personal prejudices. Relatives much of the time expose children to slanderous, racial or ethnic comments. In the event that parents are genuine in their principles, they ought to stand up and let their views be known. Overlooking these remarks and slurs is the same as supporting them.

It is additionally critical for parents to tell their children why they oppose biased comments. Youngsters ought to be told promptly how wrong for such remarks are and how frightful they can be. Likewise, parents ought to do the following:

- o Accept each of your children as unique individuals and let them realize that you perceive and value their qualities.

- o Make a firm decision that no individual ought to be excluded or teased on the premise of race, ethnicity, sex, disabilities, religion or age.

- o Provide your children with chances to connect with individuals of various racial, ethnic and religious crowds.

- o Provide open doors for children to find out about distinctive individuals through books or projects that give bits of knowledge of different societies.

o Help children recognize stereotyping, preference and segregation. A few parents feel, discussing these issues will just expand their child's attention to them and advance bias.

o Teach children how to stand up to schoolmates who are preferential with instant reactions.

II.

Teaching Our Children Tolerance:

Racism continues to rear its ugly head in diverse forms; from religion to politics, to ethnicity, to gender, and so much more. And it has stretched us apart and limited us from achieving our set goals. But the big question is: should we continue to fold our arms and watch our world fall apart or should we get involve and take a stand?

Our interaction with multicultural society differs. Some of us are quite comfortable with it while others are not. It is consequent upon our interaction with different kinds of people.

Tolerance is not about accepting bad behaviour, but accepting "people" for who they are and treating those how "you" wish to be treated. Tolerance comes in at this juncture, and the need to incorporate it in our children is necessary. It is imperative that our children learn from other cultures. It opens their eyes to new ideas, capacities and experiences. There is so much to learn from other cultures, and if tolerance can be used as a platform, it could open doors to new businesses, educational opportunities, travel, lifestyle and so much that we never imagined.

For our children to make a success out of their life, they must work with others. It is essential they step away from their comfort zone and make a move to learn more about others and appreciate them for who they are. This step is quite critical and can be productive if done right.

This is what tolerance is all about—accepting people in spite of their shortcomings and treating them the way you would rather be treated. It is pertinent your children know about this fact now and rather than later.

Don't get me wrong, I'm not saying sacrifice your heritage and beliefs—no, hold on to those beliefs 100%---but celebrate the differences you find in others.

Tolerance level with parents speaks volume and sends a loud message to their children. Know for a fact that your children will pick up whatever tolerance level you have because they look up to you for guidance and support.

When you as a parent display tolerance as regards to your actions when it comes to other cultures, you're invariably sending out a strong message and your children will imitate and learn from it.

Give your children the opportunity to develop close friendships with people of different races. Teach your children to accept people as individuals. Teach them that there is no room for bigotry. Remember that our children are influenced by the world around them. Examine your own attitudes and opinions about those of a different race. Before stereotyping people, stop and think what your stereotyping is doing to your children and the world around them.

By so doing, you're living by example and making it easier for your children to mingle and learn from other culture. That creates an atmosphere of openness towards other cultures.

There has to be a practical experience in the combination; children need to have a first-hand account of people who are similar to them and how they can contribute to their lives.

Here are some guidelines for teaching your children tolerance:

o Consider seriously, the way you speak with other people. You'll have to ensure that there is an element of tolerance when talking to others. Make it a point of duty to demonstrate in front of your children the act of respecting other people by reflecting it on your attitude daily.

o As parents, guardians, or caregivers be mindful of the words you use around your children because they are fast learners and as such they are quite attentive. Children can joke around with slang names associated with different groups, and most of these slangs were learned from the home front.

o Be mindful of the words you utter when having a conversation with your spouse because your children could be listening. Make sure you talk about positive things

22

about different groups with facts to back them up; desist from name-calling at any point in time.

o There is every possibility your children may pick up what they have heard from the home front and repeat in other private settings outside of the home.

o Ensure every question directed at you by your children is answered appropriately, in the most honest and respectful way. Your children will notice differences in people; discuss them in a respectful way.

o Select movies, stories, and games that projects differences in persons in a positive light. What your children watch can have a severe impact on their line of thought. If they watch some movies that has a prejudice tone, make sure you discuss it with your children and how the future pain can be for those people.

o When you model tolerance and respect in your home, expect your children to learn from you. Make it clear that disrespectfulness is unacceptable either in the house or outside.

o The differences between your family members should be valued in totality. Accept everybody's shortcomings either regarding lifestyle, interest, or abilities. It will be great if you could help your children feel that sense of value in whatever they do.

o Create an avenue for self-esteem in your family unit. When you don't show respect for others, it deprives you of your happiness and you feel less secure. Let your children know that respect is reciprocal.

o Let your children be actively involved in matters regarding diversity either at school, in sports, in the community, or at camp and so many other places.

o Make it easy for your children to learn about other cultures and traditions. Explore the differences and similarities when it comes to the celebration of festivities with other cultures; talk about the experience and share with your children.

o Teach family traditions to your children in a sensible way and instigate the sense of pride in them. Be wise enough to show where you

o belong and teach others what you have to offer.

Taking all things together, how we feel about others is significantly an immediate impression of our most profound sentiments about ourselves. Clear understanding, tolerance, and fairness, bring to the fore-front our self-image as a nation. It is a known fact that in spite of the differences in race, color and religion, Americans still leave in peace, respecting others' beliefs and values. This legacy

should be encouraged among our children. Make sure you play your part by being a good role model to your children.

If we can collectively put all hands on deck, we will be taking a giant leap forward in the actualization of this lofty goal. And it can be done, if we stay true to ourselves and committed to the goal that lies before us.

Chapter 3

All Lives Matter

For many Americans, especially those of color, racism is a reality of everyday life. Not only are people of color more likely to be attacked and assaulted, but they also have to face discrimination every single day of their lives.

Have we as society deviated from where our founding fathers stated in the Declaration of Independence[2] these immortal words, "We hold these truths to be self-evident, that all men are created equal, that they are endowed by their Creator with certain unalienable Rights, that among these are Life, Liberty and the pursuit of Happiness" these words lay the foundation that America stands on.

---

[2] The Declaration of Independence:
http://www.archives.gov/exhibits/charters/declaration_transcript.html

Humanity ability to relate and get along with each other in peace and perfect harmony is essential, if we are to survive as a people. We must learn how to treat and interact with one another and begin the process of building bridges instead of walls. It's no secret that in the midst life challenges, there will be disagreements and misunderstandings among cultures. Although we may disagree at times, there should never be any bitterness or hatred towards one another.

The world today presents a different picture from what it was at the beginning of the 20th century. Enormous and incredible changes brought about in various facets of life due to scientific advancement have touched upon the lives of all people of all races. Similar information on the ways of life of other people, now instantaneously reach all parts of the globe giving scope for reaction, assimilation, adoption, or adaptation. Although many concede the existence of exceptional bigots, few acknowledge the persistence of a structure that systematically apportions opportunities and life chances along distinctly racial and gendered lines. Despite copious evidence indicating worsening or unimproved patterns of discrimination and violence toward people of color, many white people and some people of color believe that these discriminatory institutional practices are related to America's past.

The big question, that is often asked "why the killings?" Why can't we exercise racial tolerance and live together as one? No race deserves marginalization or being mistreated, not to talk of killing one another.

On the evening of November 13, 2015, the world experienced the barbaric act of some men who found it hard to tolerate others' religious affiliations or belief---the shocking terror attacks in Paris [3]shook the world to its foundation. And on the morning of March 22, 2016 in Brussels, Belgium three coordinated attacks throughout the city claimed the lives of 32 people plus the 3

---

[3] 2015 Paris Terrorists Attacks http://www.cnn.com/2015/12/08/europe/2015-paris-terror-attacks-fast-facts/index.html

terrorists and injured over 300 people in a terrorist attack.[4] And on the morning of June 12, 2016, at an night club in Orlando, Fla. [5] a lone gunman Omar Mateen shot and killed 49 people and wounded 53 others. His motives are still unknown but his attack has left a nation mourning and asking why.

New stories surface daily in regards to violence and senseless killing of men, women, and children of all races, this reminds us of the ever presence of the social evil called racism and its associated consequences. African-Americans and people of different race, religion, creed, and sexual preference are often at the receiving end of this evil through police brutality, bigotry, injustice, marginalization or dehumanization, genocide, and murder.

There is a lot of hatred in this world and incidents of racial violence, discrimination, injustice, and intolerance have caused so much

---

[4] 2016 Brussels bombings https://en.wikipedia.org/wiki/2016_Brussels_bombings
[5] Orlando Night Club Shooting: http://www.msnbc.com

pain in the world today and deserve to be mentioned. We have normalized these issues against the human race and taken them for granted--as human dignity is thrown out of the window and self-gratification embraced to the detrimental of other people or their race.

As if that is not enough, the flagrant disregard for human lives continues with the act of dehumanization, where another individual is considered less of a person and fueled by the fact that he or she is of a different race. This act has been used to justify aggressive actions of some groups towards another throughout history. For instance in the 30's and 40's Nazi Germany used propaganda movies and posters depicted Jews as a rat. Quite a number of people who were against the abolition of the slave trade liken African-Americans to apes. If these groups realized that all lives matter, they wouldn't clutch to the propaganda of dehumanization.

For the last few years, researchers have concentrated their effort at measuring indirect forms of dehumanization. In 2006, psychologist Susan Fiske [6]took it upon herself to conduct a test on how peoples' brains react to images of addicts and the homeless. Her discovery was strong neutral signs of disgust, supporting the theory that dehumanization could be associated with the human race. But we can do away with such belief and live a much more inclusive life with our fellow man.

Don't get me wrong, this chapter is never in support of any race with respect to their actions or inactions, but to make a case for the violence, the killings, the bigotry, marginalization or dehumanization among all races of the world must be brought to a halt.

For us to combat this monster called racism, we must all unite—whether black, white, red, brown, or yellow —and work together as a unit in love, peace and harmony. That way, we will appreciate and respect each other's beliefs and make good of our common goal.

---

[6]Psychologist Susan Fiske https://fiske.socialpsychology.org

The lives of every individual on the face of this earth matter, and it's only when this is established in the hearts and minds of the human race, can we then begin to respect one another and value life. It might be a difficult task, though, but with a committed effort and determination on our part, something worthwhile can be achieved.

No matter the color of your skin, social status, or level of education, we are all equal in God's eyes, and why won't you matter in the eyes of your creator? As long as we shy away from the truth, issues such as race, gender inequality and so much more will continue to be a big problem.

Let it be known that all lives matter and let's join hands together and achieve this lofty goal. But whether you like it or not, race or color difference is overlooked by God, what matters is you, yes, your life matter. My life matter and all lives matter. This is what it means to be made in the image and likeness of God, as the Word of God tells us in the Book of Genesis 1:27 *"So God created man in his own image, in the image of God created he him;*

male and female created he them."—everyone, whether you're black, white, brown, red, yellow, male, straight, bisexual, transgender, young, middle-aged, or mature, we all matter, as every life matters!

Chapter 4

Is Being Black A Crime?

As a nation, we have progressed in science and technology, but have fallen behind when it comes to race relations. We still judge individuals based upon the color of one's skin and not by their character.

Why does skin color matter? That is a serious question for our nation to answer. For instance African-Americans will tell you they have been victimized times without number because of the color of their skin, and their experiences as black people leave much to be desired. For instance my African ancestors were stripped of all they had—their homes, culture, identity, religion, and families---because they were black; you begin to wonder if being black is a crime. The dehumanization did not end there. A large number of them were packed into ship hulls en-route to an unknown land and so many lost their lives en-route to this land called America and other parts of the world. Being black should come with so much dignity in spite of the dehumanizing treatments melted out to our ancestors which remain symbolic in the annals of history.

A vast majority of my ancestors were sold off on auction blocks like live stock or property, all because of the color of their skin. The enslavement of black people was not the only thing that the white slave masters did to them, their women were raped countless number of times. Some of the African men were whipped, castrated, burned, and lynched to death simply because they were blacks. They were dehumanized and seen as property and treated as non-human being, they were denied justice and protection under the law, and in the long run, they were even put to death for no just cause.

Black Businesses were forced to close down because the owners were black—even black schools, black universities, and black churches were not left untouched, as they were bombed and burned down.

When you put all these inequalities into perspective, all you get is a deep-seated wound that is embedded in the hearts, souls, and mind of a people which depicts pain and sorrow and will forever be a constant reminder of the harrowing experience of what our ancestors had to pass through and what many of us face today at the hands of the oppressor.

Because society treats these issues with levity, the wound has now formed a scar and has created a barrier, limiting the advancement of African-Americans in this nation.

You must develop a thick skin to accommodate all the criticisms and negativities that surround being an African-American. Our survival instinct has always been there to act as our support system to our dual status as blacks and the less important citizen in the predominately white society. We are not unmindful of racism and bigotry that has been extolled to greater heights in recent times, but we must continue to forge ahead and make our voices heard.

Denying the obvious fact that stares us in the face would tantamount to supporting the myth of those who holds a contrary view. As blacks, the sufferings and pains melted out to us are in their numbers. Our hearts have been ripped apart; we have been used as an object of entertainment, often times hope was lost; yet our voices of pain suppressed. We have been stripped of our clothing, unfed, and made to feel inferior. We have been reduced to subhuman beings at the hands of the white oppressor.

As W.E.B. Du Bois stated in his book "The Souls of Black Folk" [7]suppose after all, the world is right and we are less than men? Suppose this mad impulse within is all wrong, some mock mirage from the untrue? This type of thinking and course is wrong and will not be beneficial toward being victorious over a turbulent past.

---

[7] W.E.B. Du Bois: The Souls of Black Folk

The oppressor might have taken a lot from us, but one thing remained, our faith in God Almighty and the fact that we trust in Him to make a way for us.

Additionally, they have also found it difficult to divest us of the fact that we are black and proud. Though we have suffered immense hatred and untold hardship, we still have the courage and strength to move on irrespective of what has been thrown at us from time immemorial. You might wonder where this strength and courage emanated from. Our parents made it a point of duty to instill in us to trust in God during the time their families were being separated and sold to a new owner and this has been demonstrated in our "black spirituals;" [8] as it reinforces encouragement, codes and messages of a black people whose struggles and despair unfolds their existence.

Coming together under one body in Church when they could hear encouraging preaching and singing, were all that was needed to strengthen the

_____

[8] Black Spirituals http://www.negrospirituals.com

bond among them and by extension, kept all hope alive in their hearts and minds.

I'm black and proud and on top of that a fervent believer in Jesus Christ and I have taken Him as my Lord and Savior, and by the power of His spirit, I have been able to discard the hatred and anger and purge myself of the "score to settle" mentality with people of the Caucasian background. The younger generation has got a lot to learn from what will be passed on to them. And if they can imbibe these teachings, it will actually put them in a good position for better days ahead.

According to Mark Twain[9], "when some group of people is enslaved, what is paramount at that instance is to make the world see them as being less of a human. The next task is to entrust upon his fellow countryman a feeling of inferiority complex and also make the man actually believe he is inferior." The mentality of the black man in this nation has suffered so much degradation and dehumanization that he has been made to see

---

[9] Mark Twain "The Adventures of Huckleberry Finn"

himself as being inferior. The whites have categorically made it clear that "God and "nature" made a costly mistake when the black race came to be. Being black is now been greeted with so much disdain to the extent that various parts of society are now disassociating itself from anything black—or colored or Negro.

Negro is a word for black in Spanish; it has been grossly misunderstood. The word is never stated in good English even though it seems like it may be intimated or suggested. A Negro may feel offended if described as black. An Irishman once told me that I offend him by referring to myself as a Black man. He tried to clarify by saying that I'm actually brown not black, but in return, I also let him know that he is not actually white either.

The simple fact that white regard themselves as "white" makes a strong statement and extol all that is white, only for these same whites to downgrade people of African heritage when they referred to themselves as "black."

It is time to break this shackles that has caused us so much pain and wounded our souls. African-American must brace up to the challenge and unite in brotherly love. Love is essential at covering up the scars caused by racism. Let's face it, it's a tough task to achieve and by no means an overnight process; it will certainly take some time. In book of Psalms it acknowledges the fact that time heals all wounds.[10] It is an immense gift from God which is helping us heal wounds and restore hope to an otherwise troubled world.

As the wounds of racism run deep, cutting across generations, but there is always the hope of healing and restoration, so long as there are willing souls among us, whose hearts are full of love than hate.

---

[10] Psalms 147:3 (KJV)

Chapter 5

Racism In America

America has not changed much since the days of Dr. Martin Luther King Jr. and the civil rights struggle[11]of the 50's and 60's, as we are fighting the same battles then but perhaps tougher ones today, such as the ongoing rise of poverty, violence, racial discrimination, economic injustice, social injustices, inequality, police brutality, division, hunger, violations of political freedoms, terrorism as well as basic liberties, extensive neglect of the interests and rights of women, and worsening threats to our environment and to sustainability of our economic and social lives.

Racism is a cancer that feeds off of fear, division, hatred, prejudice, discrimination, isolation, disunity and anything that will cause people to separate from uniting with others.

---

[11] Dr. Martin Luther King, Jr. and The Civil Rights Movement:
http://www.thekingcenter.org/movement-intensifies

Racism in America is a consuming sickness creating barriers that's destroying our nation instead of uniting us for the common good. We as Americans should be better than this. As America is the leader in the world and all eyes tend to fall upon us as we lead the world in moral matters.

However, people are less concern about voting or having their rights protected. Poverty is on the rise as the rich are getting richer from the sweat and tears of those who have no voice or determination to rise above their circumstances. War has become a profit making business that the rich get richer and the poor goes off to fight for something they know nothing about, but are the real victims of greed and deception.

Racism is an evil that divides our nation by pitting one race against another, therefore causing division, with no form of building a better bridge of unity that will link us together.

Violence is on the rise because we feel we cannot get along with one another, so it's best to try to destroy one another or those whom we feel do not look like us nor agree with us.

Although the United States is a wonderful nation with unlimited freedoms and opportunities and I love this country and I value what it means to be an American. But let's face it, whether you think America is the greatest country in the world or not. There are qualities that make America a great nation, but there are a number of challenges which we still face, and will continue to face, that is sending our nation down a road of mediocrity.

America needs a new direction with clear minded thinkers, who aren't afraid to speak the truth and tell our nation that it has lost its way and that it needs to take a different path to avoid further destruction, such as violence, war, hatred, discrimination, greed, and destruction. The need for bridges is more evident now than ever before, bridges bring people together and connect them for the common good to work through our differences to build unity.

The world looks to this nation for guidance and direction, but when a certain group of people in this nation gets into their minds that the hands of time needs to go backward to a time when it was common for one race of people to conquer, dominate, enslave, dehumanize, mistreat, deny the basic human rights of another, and murder them because of the color of their skin. They have not learned the advantage when people of different races can come together for the common good of all of mankind.

In a country where our discourse is divided and now scattered into a spider web of varying political ideologies, we are faced with a great deal of political and psychological issues: some are important while others are more important. Addressing these issues promptly would allow the United States to continue to lead the world by example, and inevitably restoring our nation to what once made it great.

Yet, with all of the progress made, our nation still fails to address the race issue which has plagued our society for decades. It has been said that prejudice is America's unique sin. Furthermore, today, very much into our nation's third century, we are a long way from being free of it. Separate-yet-equal is no more the tradition that must be adhered to, yet for so many individuals, it is still an unavoidable truth. African-Americans are lopsidedly influenced by poverty, unemployment and insufficient food. Black family units have under one-tenth the wealth of white families, by and large. A large number of black, brown and poor youngsters are consigned to under-resourced and struggling schools.

We cannot downplay police brutality. Where is our nation going when these racial acts are still happening on our streets? For instance, in the St. Louis suburb, on the streets of Chicago, Los Angeles and many others across America, blacks and other people of color continually face embedded racism and second-class treatment. The political leaders have not brought desired change; they have failed to curb extreme policing and imprisonment rates or create economic opportunities and bring about hope.

While the term "police brutality" is typically connected with the setting of bringing about physical mischief, it might likewise include psychological damage through the utilization of intimidation strategies past the extent of an authoritatively endorsed police method. In the past the individuals who occupied with police brutality may have acted with certain endorsement of the local legal system, amid the Civil Rights era. In the current period people who engage in instances of police brutality may do as such with the implicit endorsement of their bosses or they may be racist officers; in either case they may execute their activities under the shade of the law, and as a rule take part in a subsequent cover-up of their unlawful activity.

Undoubtedly, the eminence of race relations is obvious from the volatile combination of perplexity and resentment that portrays open verbal confrontation. Both sentiments emerge from a profound abyss of understanding that now isolates blacks and whites. Numerous whites have turned out to be progressively hateful of blacks, and passionately dismiss racial inclinations. Most blacks, by contrast, bolster governmental policy regarding minorities in society as key to battling the persevering impacts of white racism.

On the other hand, from the Los Angeles riots to the O.J. Simpson case, blacks and whites appear to see one another over an unfriendly gap. There is a political gorge too: progressively the Republican's party is turning into the gathering of whites, while the Democratic Party is obliged to its African American voting base. On the off chance that these political and racial divisions are exacerbated, we are liable to witness a further disintegration of the bonds that holds our nation together. In this manner, America's generally exceptional endeavor to develop a really multiracial society may be bound to come up short.

To reduce various forms of racial discrimination and prejudice, it is critical that we keep advancing forward with the necessary legal reforms. In any case, past history reveals that we truly cannot legislate an end to prejudice. People must address racism in their personal relationships within their hearts and in their daily lives. Racism must be challenged in our thinking, workplace, institutions, the media, and in every facet of our society.

Generally, our culture was drafted by the upper stratum of society. In any case, that is not true. One unique thing about our common culture is that it is not something fabricated exclusively by the upper stratum of society. It holds truths that all Americans can perceive and think for themselves. These truths are gone from era to era: in the family, our classrooms and in religious institutions.

Our common culture stays solid and sound and it will remain so as long as its fundamental ideologies are transmitted to future generations. One approach to do this is through the educational system. Here we can sharpen our children's understanding of America, its history, embedded opportunities and obligations of citizenship in a free society.

Americans don't have a typical ancestry and or a typical bloodline. What we share in like manner is a system of laws and convictions that molded the foundation of this nation. Our society won't make do without the values of tolerance. What's more, cultural tolerance adds up to nothing without our diverse cultural understanding. The challenge confronting America will be the shaping of a common culture. In the event that we surrender the ideal of America as a plural country, we've deserted the very intent America represents.

America can be proud of its great leader, the 44thPresident of the United States, the Honorable Barack H. Obama[12], who has demonstrated tremendous courage and wisdom in leading this nation to a better way of life across all racial and political lines. His bold leadership and progressive policies have moved this nation from financial ruin to prosperity. In him many have become inspired to recognize that we need real change and that it's going to take all of us united in true brotherhood and sisterhood for the purpose of moving our country forward.

Many Americans across this country are waiting patiently for our nation to come together in peace, love, and unity. We may never reach that point any time soon and it may seem like a farfetched dream, but together we must find the means. We must create a safe and secure

---

[12] Barack H. Obama: https://en.wikipedia.org/wiki/Barack_Obama

environment for our children and our children's children.

We must realize that America is a family. And in a family there will be disputes and differences, but in our family we must not let it break us into pieces. We have to discover our strengths in our diversities. We have to battle racism and dispose of it for the last time and bring our nation together in unity, peace, and love. But it's going to take great men and women who are willing to stand up and be counted to do their part to change our world.

The struggle is far from over. Discrimination and racial hatred continue to be a problem to this day. For some in this nation they choose hate over love because it's easier to hate your fellowman than to love him, because with hate it's effortless and require no intelligence. But to love requires one to dig deep within themselves and place their heart on the line.

If enough of us would come together for the common good of humanity and work to change our world and make it a better place for all of humanity. We can then began to see a positive change in our world that will over shadow all racial hatred that currently exist.

Now is the time for all of us who care enough to step forward and do their part to bring about a change in this nation, once and for all, "Now is the time"....

Chapter 6

Institutional Racism

Institutional racism refers to a form of racism which has been established in social and political institutions. It happens when institutions, organizations or governments discriminate, either indirectly or deliberately, against particular groups of individual to restrict their rights.

This sort of racism is a reflection of the assumptions of the racist group so that the practices of this group are regarded as the norm which other groups should align with. It systematically and regularly gives advantage to some cultural and ethnic groups and marginalizes other groups and puts them at a disadvantage.

Institutionalized racism denies racial group, usually considered as inferior to a dominant race group, equitable access to education, justice, medical care, housing, politics etc. It is a form of discrimination based on race that has been established as a normal attitude within an institution, organization or society.

When we consider Institutional racism in the school environment, most times what readily comes to mind is the idea of sitting at the back of the bus, separate bathrooms, and demeaning remarks made to students of some religious or ethnic minority.

However, institutional racism is a bigger problem in schools today, though it may not be easily seen, the effects are however the same. In the year 1998 a school teacher in the United States by name Evelyn Hanssen wrote a book titled, "A White Teacher Reflects on Institutional Racism[13]." In her book, she narrated many different instances where institutional racism occurred which she felt had enormous effect on both the students and the school environment: even though many of them may not even realize it.

Racism experienced by students of an institution of learning could lead to lower

---

[13] Evelyn Hanssen "A White Teacher Reflects on institutional Racism"

educational outcomes and early school dropout. Discrimination in employment could also lead to lesser employment opportunities and a higher rate of unemployment for such students when they graduate from school. This further leads to lower income levels and discrimination in the supply of goods and services, restricted access to health care, housing, and opportunities in life.

Our society as a whole plays a significant part in permitting racism to become an endemic part of it. Governmental institutions in America make racism legitimate in one way or the other by enacting laws which are targeted at people from a particular race, age, ethnic origin or social class even though this may not be specifically stated or obvious. This sort of discrimination over a period of time causes the general population to feel less concern over others because the government has allowed such segregation to linger in its efforts to eliminate criminality in any form it feels should be prioritized at any point in time. Whenever young black people or any institution representing them claims racism, it would be seen as a mere excuse to allow people deny responsibility for their actions.

Some studies into the reasons why most police officers in the United States carry out stop and search and who their targets are reveal the bias of the police toward age groups, ethnic groups and particularly towards race groups. The reasons officers give for stops included dress, appearance, ethnicity, vehicle, and age. Other reasons include location, behavior, and any information available. Further research also showed that although sometimes, young black men may be stopped disproportionately by police officers, in certain areas they could be under represented by police officers in stops. The research also claimed that police officers over-represent white people in stops. The Asians were less likely to be stopped than either whites or blacks, although there were some exceptions.

Hence, depending on the nature of the research and maybe the sort of questions asked to police officers and those mandated to stop when they are asked to, ethnic minorities may have to deal with less or more bias by police officers when it has to do with stop and search procedures.

The most difficult form of racism to recognize and conquer is institutional racism, especially when it is propagated by governments and institutions who do not consider themselves to be racist. This type of racism further consolidates the marginalization already experienced by some groups in the same community.

To adequately respond to the challenges created by institutional racism in the United States, newer and comprehensive solutions and strategies are required. Industries and businesses can better respond to the problems caused by institutional racism by consolidating the support for affirmative action goals to hire, advance and promote the most qualified individuals, without regards to race.

Black men and black women can respond better and more effectively to the challenges created by institutional racism by working in unity with each other with the aim of creating and developing new opportunities for success. This can be achieved by investing talent and money to develop and patronize businesses owned by black people which create jobs, provide essential business services to the black community, and also be a symbol of pride which will represent what black people can do for themselves and by themselves

Chapter 7
Why The Confederate Flag Needs To Come Down

The history of the Confederate Flag; Many flags of the confederate's states of America were made use of during its existence from 1861-1865. Today, three states whose flags are based upon the confederate flag are Mississippi, Georgia and Tennessee. The one of North Carolina derived its base on the state 1861 flag, which when traced back appeared to be from the first confederate flag. Dating back to the end of the American civil war, the use of confederate flags and its sorts for personal or official use has been existing with some political, cultural and racial controversy. The rebel flag which is an acknowledge symbol of the South though historically have not represented the

Confederate States of America (CFA) as a nation, is a merge of the battle flags color with the second Navy Jack's design. The second confederate Navy Jack has a rectangular predecessor of the battle flags it was flown only on confederate ships during 1863-1865. The battle flag which in a wider note referred as the battle flag of the confederacy form the basis of more than 180 independent military flags.

The confederate flag received its popularity at the first half of the 20th century, but at World War II some U.S military identified with some comprising a large number of Southerners assumed the flag were their unofficial symbol. This flag was first raised by marine from what was termed the self-styled Rebel Company which is made up of 1st Battalion and 5th Marines. It was seen from a distance but was taken down three days later by General Simon B. Buckner, Jr. who says that it was unsuitable. After a complaint filed by African-American soldiers, the use of that flag by soldiers was put into investigations which made the rebel flag to be barely used by the military, though unofficially it's still flown by soldiers. The rebel flag in the early 21st century has become a symbol of division in the United States, this is because, a survey conducted in 2015 across all the races reveals that a good number of Americans are of the opinion that the second confederate Navy Jack represented Southern worth, rather racist; while a similar past survey in 2000 has almost the same results. The survey result from the South was entirely different in which a wider percentage of equal results was obtained from the South. In the results, the White Southern are of the view that it's a symbol of pride while the Black Southern are of the opinion of racism.

There has been a lot of panic, trauma and emotional disturbance at the slightest display of the rebel flag due to the argument over its symbolism. Those who are in the supporting side of the flag see it as a symbol of freedom of clearly cultural tradition of the South in the hands of the oppressive Northern government, also in the view of some schools prohibiting it as a racist emblem. This is widely felt by African-Americans because they see it as an open symbol of racism by the Southern states after the end of the attempt to resolve the problem in late 1870s.

In 2005 research carried out by two western Carolina University, found out that over 70% of African-Americans voted for the removal of the flag from the South Carolina State House to the white Southerners who perceive the flag as a symbol of heritage without any racial or political involvement. As a result of this varying understanding, there is a lot of controversy over the use of this flag in southern states flags at some events and public structures. The issue of this confederacy flag have remain one of the most serious and heated debates among many Southern state legislatures over its civic position since 1990s. It was passed as a bill to pull down this flag on early 2000 from the state house dome of South Carolina State with a majority vote favoring its removal. The flag has been removed from the peak of the state house and placed on a commemorative platform on the front lawn of the capitol but the available state law stops it removal from the ground of the state house without further legislation.

Some reasons have been pointed out by people why the rebel flag needed to come down, these includes; the original nature of the design. It was designed with white which shows white supremacy, as the designer of one version, William Thompson stated in his reason for motivation that "their fight is to maintain the heaven foresay supremacy of the white to the minor colored race, a white flag will then be symbolically of our cause" he went further to say that the flag will be honored as white man's flag by the civilized world. The flag wasn't an official flag of the white during the civil war as people believed. It has shown that the rebel flag wasn't flown over South Carolina's capitol till 1962-as it was recognized then by the civil rights movement. There was claim by the pro-flag supporters that the civil war was about states right not slavery. Among all these reasons that has been stated above on why the rebel flag should be removed, the most disheartening incident that has to lower the flag down in South Carolina is the killing and shedding of blood of innocent people by the white supremacist.

One of the most horrendous incident in the history of this nation happened on June 17, 2015 at Emmanuel African Methodist Episcopal Church in Charleston, SC. [14] Where nine African-Americans worshipers were slain, among the dead includes State Senator Clementa Pinckney[15], the 41 years old Pastor of the church were all killed by a gunman named Dylann Roof during a Wednesday night prayer service. This incident was considered a hate crime and struck the nation at its core and race relations again came into view.

After a thorough investigation of the gunman background, it was discovered that he was not only a white supremacist but a supporter of the confederate flag philosophy. It took the death and

---

[14]Emmanuel African Methodist Episcopal Church:
http://www.emanuelamechurch.org
[15] State Senator Clementa Pinckney:
https://en.wikipedia.org/wiki/Clementa_C._Pinckney

blood of nine innocent people for the people of South Carolina to realize that it was time to remove the flag once and for all and began the process of healing for the state and the nation as a whole.

A similar incident took place in 1963, when the 16th Street Baptist Church in Birmingham [16]was bombed claiming the lives of four young innocent African American girls again innocent blood was spilled.

In conclusion, the removal of this flag will go a long way to healing all wounds created by racism and bring harmonization as President Barack Obama said, "the removal of the flag is a signal of good will and healing, and a meaningful step towards a better future."Together we can end prejudice. Our fight against racism cannot be won while there are still attitudes like the one demonstrated that fatal day in Charleston, SC.

Days after that fatal shooting, on July 10, 2015, after over fifty-four years, the confederate

---

[16]16th Street Baptist Church:
https://en.wikipedia.org/wiki/16th_Street_Baptist_Church_bombing

flag finally came down at the state house in Columbia, South Carolina marking a milestone towards healing and restoration. We have to move beyond the flag and racism and embrace the reality of brotherhood as we unite in harmony. As the doors, of a bright and productive future is set before us, let us join hands and walk therein with hope and expectation of a better day and a positive future.

Chapter 8

I Am My Brother's Keeper

When the love for God diminishes from the hearts of mankind, so does the love for one another. This statement seems to ring true as I listen to the hate rhetoric that is spewing through our air waves and across this nation. We are no longer a society striving to promote love, peace, unity, and universal brotherhood, but a society destine to destroy itself with hate.

How can a society correct the menace of racism? Is it possible for it to be corrected? Nobody can alter history or eradicate the evils of what was committed in the past. Nevertheless, there is a legacy of racism that lives on in today's world. In many respects, it is invisible, yet it is like an insidious energy that changes the atmosphere of an environment after an argument has taken place. Everyone can in one way or the other feel the tension in the air, with each person responding to it in a different way, shaping his or her attitude, either consciously or unconsciously.

Sometimes in life, you're confronted with moments of unutterable fulfillments which cannot by any means be explained by those symbols we call words. Their meaning can only be vividly expressed by the inaudible language of the heart. Such is the moment I'm experiencing. I experience this joy-filled moment not for myself alone, but for the collective groups of those devotees of nonviolence that have decided to embrace peace in the face of racial injustice, and who have acquired a new estimate of their own human worth. A large majority of them are young and cultured. Others are of the middle-aged and have remained resolute to unite and embrace peace.

If God has created us in His own image, there is no need for racial segregation or injustice. I particularly salute the courage of those that have remained united in the quiet conviction that suffering indignity is better than accepting segregation in humiliation.

I'm a fervent believer in the power of love, unity, and peace, as a means to defeating racism. Did I hear you say how? Yes, it is possible only if we try. As daunting as this challenge could be, even impracticable you might want to add, I still hold this opinion close to my heart as a viable means to defeating this social evil.

If the modern man can bring the whole world to an awe-inspiring threshold of the future, by attaining new and unfathomable peaks of scientific success, then there is hope to crush this monster known as racism. If the modern generation can produce machines that think and instruments that peer into limitless ranges of interstellar space, then there is hope to nip this evil in the bud. The human race has built bridges that transcend across the sea and airplanes that have dwarfed distances; these are scientific feats accomplished by man over the years.

In spite of these giant strides in science and technology, there is something missing--the poverty of the spirit; this is in contrast to our scientific and technological milestones. We have become richer materially, but morally and spiritually poor. We are adept at flying in the air just like birds and also swim proficiently like fish, but we have simply not learned the art of living together like brothers.

Let me not give you a false impression. The problem confronting us today is immense. It is a long way to go before the dream of freedom becomes a reality. Putting it in a figuratively biblical language, we have decided to leave behind the dusty soils of Egypt and crossed the Red Sea whose waters had been hardened for so many years by the piercing winter of massive resistance. And before we get to the majestic shores of the Promised Land, the wilderness lies ahead. It is certain that the desire to unite and show love to your neighbor in the face of racism will face prodigious hilltops of opposition and massive resistance. But with firm determination and patience, we will keep pressing on until every valley of despair is taken to new heights of hope and mountains of irrationality are brought low by humility.

The day humanity begins to understand we are made in God's image and by extension one in the sight of God, that's when the human perspective begins to change. Imagine the accomplishments enumerated earlier, then imagine what can be achieved if the world is united without any racial prejudice-- the result will be outstanding.

I believe that love, unity, and peace can re-establish a broken community. This method seeks to implement the just laws by appealing to the large number of the majority who through fear, pride, blindness have allowed their conscience to go to sleep

Embracing this approach to solving the problem of racial injustice is not without successful precedent. It was well utilized in a magnificent way by Mohandas K. Gandhi [17]to challenge the might of the British Empire and liberate his people from political domination and economic exploitation.

---

[17] Mohandas K. Gandhi http://www.biography.com/people/mahatma-gandhi-9305898

If you can show love to your fellow man, embrace his limitations and see him as your brother, I can affirm that the ugly face of racism will be crushed in no distance time. Our personal beliefs shape our experience and those beliefs collectively shape our culture and society. It is high time we take a second look at these beliefs individually and collectively and clearly see the errors in our judgment. Correcting the menace of racism must begin with reconciling the conflict of those ideas and beliefs that gives life and energy to racism.

II.

True Brotherhood:

True brotherhood is the sincere bonding of men of diverse beliefs, backgrounds and societies around a single or set of commitments which direct their way of life.

Can the past of slavery, bigotry, prejudice, and discrimination be healed and true brotherhood achieved? What will it take before hatred takes over our world?

The idea of true brotherhood is not enough. You can say all you want; but what makes the difference is putting it into practice. Choosing to let go of judgment of others based on racial discrimination and segregation, especially at times when you do not really want to, will make you see them as brothers.

The only real form of difference you can make is to alter your perception of people back to the true perception which is based on love.

It is one thing to love your brother when they are loveable, but it is another to love them when they do not return your love. When you make a judgment that they have done something wrong or they have harmed you in a certain way, you will not be willing to show love to them. Your ego will judge them as not worthy of your love, because they have harmed you. This stems from the original separation of not being worthy of the love of God.

74

What you think that you do not have, you cannot share with others.

Regardless of where you are, if you want to see others as your brother, it starts with you making the decision to see and accept the truth. Do it always and you will see it always? Do it sometimes and you will see it sometimes? Right now, your beliefs in separation will not allow you to see through the illusions of discrimination until you take a firm decision to change your perception. Who you truly are does not hurt a brother and you do not hurt them either. It is only the ego that claims to be hurt and sparks off the flame of hatred.

In this world, we all have the same goals, needs, wants and problems as our brothers walk beside us as heavenly companions. See them with a judgmental attitude and they will behave as such. See them as Holy, and you will see the God in them reflect back to you. All that is required is your ability to change your prejudiced judgment about a brother at all times. That is what true brotherhood stands for.

Chapter 9

The Distinctive Power of Unity

"How good and pleasant it is when God's people live together in unity!" Psalm 133 (NIV)

Working together in peace, love, brotherhood, and unity is the panacea that heals all wounds both small and great. It helps us to enjoy the happy times of life. When there is oneness, there will be more strength in opinion, action and character.

In the sad moments of sickness and death, in the good moments of marriage, it is the unity and love of the well-wishers that makes the despair less and the pleasure great. This is the distinctive power of unity. A disunited community or a lone individual cannot achieve much and also cannot enjoy the benefits of any achievement. Strength is the secret power of unity, which is built on mutual faith, love, and trust for each other, and the oneness of a well thought out goal.

When individuals unite, they come or join together to form a distinct or unique unity with connections of purpose and mindset. Whenever there is a decision to be reached, it is often with the collaboration of every one member of the unit.

Hence in order to make outstanding achievement and progress, love, peace and unity are the necessary ingredients. Success is guaranteed at the end of the day, if you have a consolidated and united group working towards a goal even though your targets may be good or bad.

Imagine if the entire world would set aside all individual differences and unite together to exploit the power of unity, it would be a world where we can all make untold positive impacts.

There is enormous power and possibility when we work together in love, peace and unity. When there is unity of goal and purpose rather than division, people can achieve almost anything they are determined to do. When people are united, the contributors or members do not have to look or function alike, yet they are important, interdependent, needed and are all engaged with a purpose to reach a common goal. We are indeed strong as individuals but as a united force, we can influence our world in amazing ways.

More and more people are becoming aware of the benefits of working together in peace, love and unity. As this number continues to grow, we begin to witness tremendous positive changes all over the world. People are bringing their minds together to tackle enormous social problems that have bedeviled mankind for centuries. They are setting an clear example of how dwelling in unity can be beneficial to the world.

Unity is a word that is not talked about very often in the larger society. It represents togetherness, equality, synchronized opinions and thinking to ultimately accomplish a particular mission or goal. It is a word that can help bring us all together as one to achieve a collective responsibility.

Unity is a universal word that has the same meaning to everyone regardless or, nationality, race, or gender. It is very essential as no one can do everything on his or own. Like in a work environment, you will often require the assistance of someone else to enable you to move ahead in whatever task you are engaged in.

Unity seems to hold more importance today than ever before. There is more of a need for unity in a world where people are more reliant on the internet, social media and other forms of communication. There is more of the spirit of individuality in our world today. Although there is a place for this, we are social beings who have valuable and distinct contributions to make.

Working together in love, peace and unity is not an impossible task. We can agree to better ourselves and live our best by adhering to the true definition of living in unity. We need to live in unity with our family, friends, loved ones, neighbors and those we come in contact with.

Most importantly, dissociate yourself from those who are inclined towards division as they are unaware of what harm they do to themselves and our world.

If we could put aside our differences and work together, we could accomplish the impossible because we as a society would be united for the benefit of humanity.

Here are 4 helpful tips to encourage working and living together in Love, Peace and Unity:

1. Look for a common goal or cause and contribute your own quota to the solution. Find a need and take the lead. Be a part of it and help in providing a solution.

2. Do not allow any differences to result in prejudice. Whether it is skin color, disability or handicap, socioeconomic status or level of education, we need to make it a point of duty to treat everybody with respect as we work in love and unity.

3. Help bring about a change by working together in unity and a peaceful society.

4. Have an understanding of the true meaning of working together in peace, love and unity and be committed to walk in it every day. Be willing to play your part towards empowering others and making the world a better place.

II.

Love Is More Powerful Than Hate:

Love is the most important thing in our lives. Jesus Christ is humanity example of how much we need to love one another and ourselves. When we love God with all our heart, soul, mind and strength, we grow to recognize that everyone is part of His creation. Jesus makes it clear in St. John 13:34-35, we have a new commandment to Love One Another. We must love one another because we are loved by God; and have received that love, and live in light of it.

If you are reading this and thinking, this all sounds good, but there are some people you just can't love, regardless. We all probably felt that way at times, especially towards those who have hurt and wronged us. Keep in mind Jesus is love and Jesus loves everyone even the ones who betrayed Him, those who beat Him, and those who crucified Him. In Jesus, He loves everyone through us. It's just another example of why we must continually let Him direct our lives and control our will. Since this is God's kind of love, it comes into our life through our relationship with Him. If we want to love one another more, we need to draw closer to God.

If God's love lives inside of us, we will have this kind of love for others. This love John speaks of in 1 John 4:20-21, comes from the Greek word agape; it is the concept of a self-giving love that gives without demanding or expecting re-payment. This love is rare in the world. Such love requires the foundation of integrity, truthfulness, and unity with the absolute. Love is the sure sign of a true

Christian and Christ abiding spirit within our hearts. If Christ is living in our hearts, we will have this love for our fellow-man. The reason for this is once we have experienced God's mercy, we realize how blessed we are to have Christ in our life. In spite of our weaknesses and our short comings, His grace gives us strength to overcome hate. When we have this heavenly outlook in our hearts, we naturally love those who are not part of our family. It is this true love that is totally committed to the welfare of others.

Though, love springs forth a long-lasting relationship with God which comes from our being born of Him. If we are born of Him, and are abiding in Him, the resources for love are there. It is up to us to respond to His command with our will and whole being.

Jesus Himself said in St. John 14:6, "I am the way, and the truth, and the life": Jesus came to teach us the way and the truth and the life. So, if Jesus is in me, I have the way, and the truth, and the life, and the righteousness of Jesus, and His

Holiness, His redemption; and the love of Jesus, and His patience, and His humility living inside of me.

It's human nature to emulate those we admire most, so in getting to know Christ, we'll discover a God worthy of our whole-hearted love, and mankind will see that love in us and the power of God's Love. It is not for us to know who will choose Him and who will not, but we are called to be His witnesses. In order to fulfill that calling, we must love others enough to desire their salvation just as He does.

The truth of the words of Jesus Christ which have echoed over two thousand years are the basis upon which unity is built, but love is the bond that holds us together in His truth. With this, any person can look forward to spiritual health and growth and fruitfulness. Once we accept this we will realize that Love is more powerful than hate

Chapter 10

Racism and The Church

The one place that racism would have never been conceived to be is the Church, a place where racism thrives. The world in this 21st century has become a global village linked by improved networks of good transportation and enhanced communication technology. Yet we are still a long way to finding a logical solution of all manner of hostilities, which exist among people of different social, religious, and even cultural background. Though many organizations and groups in different countries are making a tremendous move to abolish racism of various kinds, it can still be read clearly, or the handwriting of this racism is still written with bold letters in some places. This can be forbidden in the constitution or books of the land but, it is very fresh in the hearts of men. It is so bad that the Christian community which consists of the number of people constituted by

Christ Himself to counter the evils of the world, has joined hands and embraced this ugly act called racism.

The church which is believed to be filled with Christians, meaning "Christ like" should be sensitive to this segregation attitude. The message which Jesus taught that is taken from the scriptural revelation should strongly affirms the worthiness of everyone created by the image and likeness of God.

This racism in question can be defined as a belief, theory or idea that there is a causal connection between some inherited physical traits and some certain traits of personality, intellect, religious or culture, the notion that some particular trait are superior while the others are the inferior or the minority. From this definition one can draw that racism refers to the perception that some differences between human congregations are related with the presence or unavailability of certain social accepted qualities. Its ideology also makes conclusions on people's worth on the basis of their acceptance in nonracial groupings like religious sects, linguistic groups or cultural groups. Because this ugly act called "racism" assume that one human group is better than the other in a way that show superior social or personal value, it exhibits itself in actions that negatively affects the lives of others. This is the situation when a person, who's in a position to enforce their judgment use their influence to offend others who are referred to as the inferior and even taking advantage of them. In the quest to grab the various dimensions of racist thoughts and behaviors, one should also need to understand some vital terms used in everyday discussion of this topic. Some of these term includes; race, culture, ethic group, ethnocentrism, majority/minority group and whole lots of them which is beyond mentioning here.

Right from the history of racism in America, it has been noted that the church did not play a role of the uninterested party, the Lutheran church in the United States played parts in racism that has become part of American society. The racism practiced in the United States by the Lutheran church is the same like those been portrayed by the general society within the country. Few examples are going to be sited in order to substantiate this view that is portrayed by the church, which was believed to be followers of Christ. These members of this church hailed slavery, which is a form of racism and saw no moral deviation from their stance.

In 1708, a Native American, who was the first to be documented as the first slave on record to seek unionism in the Lutheran congregation in New York City created an unsuitable situation. His church member owner reacted negatively to his acceptance by their congregation with the fear that he would lose his property. The crisis was settled when the slave promised to obey and serve his worldly master and mistress as faithfully as if he was still in darkness. Call it slavery or racism, its ugly face has been in the churches of America for ages.

Racism has torn apart the main purpose of the church, which was meant to profess Christ. It has succeeded in segregating churches from the other; in the Adventist church, this problem is not far-fetched. The Seventh-day Adventist church has been reported to be silent and insensitive when it comes to racial matters, they have been showing some discrimination, paternalism and even scorn to some members of its congregations. One of the fore standing North American church leader yield that "Adventists are still racially apart as rest of Christianity and some of the society. This is obvious that 11 o'clock Sabbath morning is the most isolated hour for Adventism in the North. He went further to state that our church is still damaged with racism and segregation. The church also pointed out what is called cultural snobbery that has been portrayed by some churches of the west. The Adventist scholars as leader in the United States couldn't absorb the fact that other Adventist from the third world has the potential of theological reflection. They simply underrated them and referred to them as theological immature. Another evidence of this racism in the Seventh day Adventist is that many conferences in the United States have been conducted in line with racial evidences.

Some churches in America have stood their ground on their fight for human rights. A good example is Charleston's Emanuel African Methodist Episcopal Church, this isn't just a church, but a strong historic icon of black dignity set against racism. This has made them and other black churches to suffer in the hands of those who considered themselves to be the superior. Some of these brutal acts are the murder of 9 innocent souls at Emanuel African Methodist Episcopal Church in Charleston, SC. Among the dead includes State Senator Clementa Pinckney, a 41 years old Pastor of the church. Emanuel Church is the oldest Black congregation in the south. Similar attacks has been occurring in black congregations, in 1963 the Baptist church of 16th street in Birmingham, Alabama was bombed and four girls who were preparing for Sunday school was murdered. In the 90's arsonists launched numerous attack on black churches in South Carolina, such racial discriminating acts was throughout that civil rights period. After the emancipation of black churches as a separate institution, the white southerners still sought to be in control over the African American's worship. They emphasized the responsibilities of the blacks to be obedient and made biblical references for the black bondage.

Blacks who were allowed to worship with whites had no say in the church affairs and they were all banished to the back of the church during worship as spectators rather than being accepted as a full member of the congregation. After the emancipation came the introduction of sharp religious mode of service. The Baptist and Methodist church joined African and European forms of religious expression to make a distinct version of worship that reminded the agony and pain of 19th century black life in United States. In all, the more the black churches became involved against racial discrimination and violence against them, the more the churches and its congregation were punished. A big question that still face many people is this, "can the church be reconciled and aid in the healing of America from racial division?"

Racism should not have a place in the church. By allowing racism to still exist in our churches today, we are tearing apart the love which is offered to Christians by the Holy Spirit which embraces without distinction in your race, cultural or ethnic background. I encourage us through the means of the Grace in the Holy Spirit to work within the context of all culture and churches to bring all to the faith of Christ and to motivate them to worshiping Him.

In conclusion, the Christian doctrine should inspire the church and motivate people to reach within themselves and change and change the world around them. Once this has occurred, our world can unite in peace, love and unity. In the second Vatican council it was noted that all men are endowed with a good rational soul and are all created by one GOD's image, we all have the same nature and origin and all been redeemed by Christ. We all enjoy the same divine calling and position and it is basic equality of all men and must be giving due recognition. There is no doubt that all men are not alike in terms of physical, moral and intellectual capacity, but all forms of social or cultural discrimination as regard to different color, sex, social conditions must be restrained as incompatible with God's design. I am quoting Pope John Paul II who said, "Faith and reason are like two wings on which the human spirit rises to the contemplation of truth; and God has placed in the human heart a desire to know the truth- in a word, to know himself- so that, by knowing and loving God, men and women may also come to the fullness of truth about themselves."[18]

---

[18] **Pope John Paul II, Fides et Ratio: On the Relationship Between Faith and Reason**

II.

Segregated Sunday:

The late Rev. Dr. Martin Luther King, Jr. once said in one of his many famous speeches that "Eleven o'clock on Sunday morning was the most segregated hour in America." If it were to be asked today if Sunday was still segregated; Our answer to that question would be a resounding YES; because nothing has really changed and Sunday morning still remains the most segregated time in America. We can work together, play together, shop together, eat together; but why can't we worship the same God together?

The reason is Racism, which is a sin, which is attributed to Segregated Sunday and it's still very prevalent in the church today. Racism is a spiritual problem which has always thrived in the church for centuries, yet it is very important to remember that the founder of Christianity, Jesus Christ, never once advocated it. As a matter of fact, His summary of the Ten Commandments broke down very simply "to love God with all your heart and soul and strength, and then to love your neighbor as yourself." He gave a perfect example about who is your neighbor in the parable of the Good Samaritan in St. Luke 10:30-37; Jesus showed beyond a shadow of a doubt that loving your neighbor is to transcend racial, social, and status barriers.

Jesus said in Matthew 7: 12; "Whatsoever you would that men should do unto you, even so do you also unto them: for this is the law and the prophets." This rule was not given for the Jewish people alone, but for all people of all races and nationalities. It is the perfect end toward which all the laws and the teachings of the Lord are directed. It requires that each one put himself in the place of the other. We do not want others to be prejudiced against us; we want them to understand us. Hence we are not to be prejudiced against others, but try to understand them. No matter what position we may find ourselves, we want to be treated with consideration, fairness, kindness, love, sympathy, and sometimes with compassion and mercy. We are, therefore, to treat others in the same manner. This is a very simple principal and easy to understand. When Christians sincerely pray about this, we will see a difference.

This is where reconciliation begins in the heart of mankind; and with people working together in an environment in which everyone has pledged their allegiance to Jesus Christ and allowing Him to speak to their hearts. If the church is going to provide a picture of reconciliation for the world to see; Christians and Non-Christians of all colors have to be pro-active. It isn't enough to walk one mile, however it will take walking two miles to make a difference in this world of ours. Jesus created the Church out of Love for us and it's up to us with Love to reach out to others. Moving forward means understanding that reconciliation stretches beyond integration or equality to a unity of spirit and purpose. Reconciliation begins with removing the "dividing wall of hostility" in one-on-one relationships. We must be Christ-like by viewing the other person as one whom God loves dearly. The time has come for believers to strive to be a role model of reconciliation in a world of bitterness and hatred between the different racial groups. This world is big enough for all of us. God is big enough for all of us and God created diversity. If we can learn from nature about life then we can learn from each other the importance of diversity.

Whether we are black, white, red, yellow, or brown, we are to unite with one another and we are to live in harmony with one another because of the fellowship we have in Christ. The future of the human race depends upon what we do now and we must work hard to preserve our existence through unity, peace, harmony and love.

Chapter 11

Black on Black Racism

African-Americans are a blessed race of people. We originated from a proud and dignified people, for this is our heritage. Our history does not begin February 1st and ends February 28th but our history opens the door to other races of people to understand and appreciate who we are and the many contributions made to the world.

We are a people that have come a long way since our ancestors were first brought to American forcibly and held captive in bondage in 1555[19]. We've broken the physical chains, resisted oppression, organized, fought, marched, disobeyed civilly and not so civilly, and forced this nation to strike down some of its most brutal and unjust laws from the ending of slavery in the 19th century

---

[19] https://en.wikipedia.org/wiki/African-American_history

to the legislation that legalized King's Holiday in the 20th century.

By most accounts today, African Americans aren't doing too well. Blacks are six times more likely to be murdered than Whites, and the majority is Black-on-Black violence. A large percentage of blacks are incarcerated and on parole than any other race, and more Black children now live in poverty than ever before.

Like the phase from a fairy tale, 'mirror mirror on the wall whose the fairest of them all,' shows us the face of our enemy, ourselves. We are a race of people that just can't seem to get ahead in life or improve our own conditions even when we have blacks in position of leadership and authority. We end up disappointed, defeated, disillusioned, and discouraged. We are a people who sabotage our own lives and the lives of others around us by not recognizing the factors that defeat us. Instead, we blame others, we blame the past, or the circumstances that have left us wounded. If our ancestors were able to keep their faith in the worst dehumanizing conditions one can ever imagine, what about us?

Of a truth, when you hear the word "Racism" being mentioned, what will hit your mind first is the dominance and superiority of the white race over other races of color. The reality however, is that people of the black race also have racist tendencies. They also have a sense of dominance and superiority over other races, including people of their own race. Whether you like it or not, the practice of black racism against fellow blacks either directly or indirectly is in existence or continues to exist.

Looking at racism from the angle of black domination, it is proven beyond a reasonable doubt and also makes it abundantly clear that apart from the whites dominating the blacks, blacks also racially abuse people of other races especially black people, whom is of their own race. For this reason, racism should be a universal term: it should not only be associated with the dominance of the whites alone.

According to the dictionary of contemporary English, Racism is defined as a belief system that one race is superior to the other. As earlier mentioned, Racism is commonly associated with the dominance and superiority of the white man over blacks. Because of this, many black persons have made countless agitations and efforts to curb this dominance and superiority. A few of these black activists include, Meager Evers, Bob Moses, Malcolm X, John Lewis, and Rev. Dr. Martin Luther King Jr. etc. These people were actively involved in the struggle to put an end to racial discrimination and segregation against black people in America.

Going by this, it would seem as though Racism in America implies only to the superiority and dominance of the white race over the black race. But that seems not to be the case in America but it also includes the discrimination of blacks over blacks.

This goes to show that people of the black race also racially abuse other blacks. Speaking about this matter without substantial evidence; waters down the issue and renders it futile. This nonsensical and irrational situation can be clearly seen when blacks do not patronize businesses owned by other blacks or support blacks in general. Blacks are mistreated by other blacks on their jobs, in their community and yes even in the church. This mistreatment stems from a form of envy, distrust, hatred that has caused a deep divide between blacks in America.

According to Willie Lynch[20], "distrust is stronger than trust, and envy is stronger than admiration, respect, or adulation." In his letter in 1712 to the slave masters, he said that if his plan of controlling black slaves is used for one year, it will make the slaves become perpetually distrustful of their own selves. His method was based on amplifying the differences among blacks using envy, distrust and fear to achieve control.

---

[20]The Willie Lynch Letter:
http://www.finalcall.com/artman/publish/Perspectives_1/Willie_Lynch_letter_The_Making_of_a_Slave.shtml

He guaranteed that if the method is applied, it will control the black slaves for a minimum of 300 years. Probably this might be the reason why there continues to be black on black racism. He also said that after the black receives this indoctrination, they shall carry on with it and become self-generating and self-refueling for hundreds to thousands of years.

Again he explains how it should be done by pitching the young black male and old black male against themselves, the light skinned slaves against the dark skinned ones, and the female versus the male. The overseers and servants must distrust all blacks but make sure that the slaves depend on and trust their masters and they must respect, trust and love them only.

One very surprising thing brought about by Willie Lynch is the extent of hate which African Americans have for their fellow African Americans in the labor market, mostly when they happen to head a supervisory role. The hatred stems from the thought that other blacks are a threat to their jobs. This has evolved so much hatred in some areas that is difficult to comprehend. How can a person honestly say that a person or group of persons are taking jobs away from him when there is no law that guarantees automatic hiring to people of any race? This sort of hatred sends a wrong signal of disunity that is passed on to future generations who then pass it on to future generations and so on.

Another thing that is also puzzling is how some blacks hate other blacks for the silliest reasons. Some blacks have been talked down on by other blacks simply because they spoke correct English and did not include the phrase "you know what I'm saying" after every other sentence, or blacks also have a problem with other blacks because they do not listen to rap music or like myself I enjoy listening to classical and opera music and I am often looked upon with disdain by other blacks.

One important fact to always remember is that no one chooses their race that he or she belongs to; but they can chose what they make of it. The discrimination of blacks against fellow blacks is alive and active. Most dark-skinned blacks are made to feel inferior about their color and many light-skinned blacks feel superior to the very dark-skinned blacks who are sometimes taunted about having very dark skin or very coarse hair.

Every adult living in the United States have the right to like whatever he/she wants to like. These things ought not to be a problem. Not everyone listens to a particular genre of music or speak in a certain way. For people to be judgmental of others of the same race just because of the music they listen to or how they speak is racism in itself.

Blacks need to understand that people should have the free will to decide who they want to be, act and talk the way they want; live the quality and class of life that they want and date whoever they want to date. People are free to pursue whatever dreams they have and live them to the fullest. We all should know that whatever is worth having is also worth working for and we should not grumble when others decide to be industrious in order to have better things in life. No one should expect things to be given freely to them, and if they have such expectations, they must be willing to accept whatever life gives to them.

When black people in American attack other black people they are only sowing seeds which lead to further division in the black community. They are in fact empowering people of other races who wish them ill. This immoral behavior hurts blacks who want the best for the black community, and it empowers those who do not wish well for black people and get pleasure when they witness blacks attacking or degrading other blacks. It is destructive, irresponsible and foolish; and the black community should recognize well enough not to behave in such a foolish manner.

This is why Black History is so important because it remind us of who we are, where we came from, and most importantly where we can go from here. This can be summed up by two very important Adinkra symbols of West Africa. The first symbol is the Sankofa. It symbolizes "the wisdom of learning from the past to build for the future" If our present generations can learn from the past then the possibility of erasing a heritage will surely be impossible.

The second Adinkra symbol is the "Ese ne tekrema" (se knee the kra-mah). This symbolizes improvement, advancement, and a need for interdependence. Many African-Americans see themselves as all right, well off, or just making it in a society that takes pride in material things over family values. However, the scene of the African-American neighborhood use to be that of harmony, neighbors knew each other, children played together on the front porches, and people were helping one another. Now a days it is a "free for all", everybody for themselves. No one looks out for the well being of their neighbors, property or family.

In St. Matthew 15:17-20 according to these verses, if we do not control our thought life, our spirit will betray us. The time has come for us as African-Americans to put away ungodly thoughts such as the hatred and jealousy we have for one another out of our mind and begin to put God first. If this becomes a problem for us, then we must make it a matter of urgent plea to God for repentance, spend more time in fellowship with others and studying the word of God. This is the only gateway by which we can save ourselves and our race from total annihilation.

To counter this manner of hatred and disunity amongst blacks is by uniting and building bridges of trust and love. This is the only thing that can bring a race that has been marginalized and abused, a race which has been programmed to be divisive and contempt towards each other. Only together in perfect harmony and peace can blacks counter the evil philosophy of Willie Lynch and embark on a new day of hope. Only then can peace, unity, and love be achieved.

Chapter 12

Who is My Neighbor?

The hatred in the world it's not of God and it's not what He wants His beautiful variety of children to display to one another. God tells us plainly that we are to love our neighbor, as we love ourselves[21]. The question is who is our neighbor? Is it just those around us that we are familiar with and have purposely surrounded ourselves with? Or have we gone outside of the box reaching out beyond our comfort zone? Jesus teaches us in the four gospels of the New Testament that we are to love one another and be in unity with them. No matter our race, nationality, language, religion, culture, social status or who's our parents or where we are located in the world.

However, we have become a selfish and uncaring society towards our fellowman. We walk

---

[21] St. Mark 12:30-31

by those who are suffering or who are in need, and we say to ourselves that's not my problem, or they are not of my race, my religion, my neighborhood, my social group, my class or my status. They are nothing to me or of anything that I am associated with so therefore that gives me the right to ignore them and to turn my back on them as I pass right on by. This type of attitude has become the norm in our society and accepted by most, but it is not of God. We are all Brothers and Sisters and are related because of a common thread, God is our Father.

The world is made of good and evil people. One who causes pain and suffering to their fellowman for no reason is not a neighbor. One who looks at wrong and decides to do nothing is not a neighbor. One who hurts or degrades the feelings of another is not a neighbor. One who lets their neighbor sleeps and lives in poverty without doing anything about the situation is not a neighbor. One who mistreats the poor with disdain and disrespect, is not a neighbor. And one who decides a person's character based upon their race and passes judgments on them, is not a neighbor.

The foundation of Christianity is based upon how one individual treats his fellowman and the love that encompasses that relationship. Which bring us to the word neighbor and the big question, who is my neighbor? The word neighbor means friend, companion, fellow citizen, and it is also similar to the word brother. Which means that it breaks down all man-made barriers and obstacles that causes separation, and disunity among mankind as well as bringing uniqueness in brotherhood. When Jesus was presented with this question, He used the parable of The Good Samaritan in St. Luke 10:29-33 to illustrate to those who lack the true meaning of the word neighbor.

The story begins with a man who had been robbed and left to perish on a road. First the priest came by who saw the man and passed by on the other side, then the Levite who also did likewise. Then the Samaritan came by, who was of a different race, different religion, and a different culture. Who looked beyond those restrictions that keep man from true brotherhood and saw that the man was in distress and without a second thought answered the call and lend a helping hand.

The Good Samaritan displayed five characteristics of a good Neighbor, 1: He saw him-You must see the needs of people and not look at their race, religion, culture, or sex but the needs of the person, **2:** He had compassion on him-You must have God's compassion on those whom you are not familiar with. **3:** He went to him-You must reach out to people and reach outside of your comfort zone. **4:** He met his needs by touching, washing, and placing oil-You must meet the need of people that are suffering and isolated. **5:** He took the time and got involved and was committed. We must take the time and get involved and be committed to helping those that are in need as the Good Samaritan.

The Samaritan's actions were a true demonstration of love because he had no prior relationship with the wounded man nor did he gain anything materially from his actions. He would instead lose time and money for his effort and the wounded man probably would not have done the same for him, if the situation were reversed. In this parable The Good Samaritan represents Christ, His pouring oil and wine in the wounds represents the ministry of Christ, while in the flesh as the salt of the earth helping a fallen mankind with the truth and the spirit of the truth. The Samaritan taking the wounded man to the inn represents Christ brining the race into the millennial conditions.

His making matters financially good with the innkeeper represents the application of the ransom merit to Divine justice for the race's deliverance and care in the millennium.

His promising to make good for any further expense called for by the care of the man wounded represents the Christ's promise of justice to make good any further claim that justice might have for men's millennial willingness.

Jesus' parable forced from the lawyer of the law to admit that the Samaritan was the real neighbor of the wounded man. Thus He helped him to see at least in part the truth that every human depending on the closeness of the relationship is neighbor to every human.

Collectively our common humanity is the neighborly bond and that only those who this bond and act accordingly are worthy of the name neighbor. The apostle Paul in his writing to the Galatians states that "As we have therefore opportunity, let us do good unto all men, especially unto them who are of the household of faith" (Gal.6:10).

Chapter 13

Weapons of Mass Destruction:

Ignorance and Fear

A lot of hatred, division and destruction exist in the world today. In the early hours of September 11, 2001[22], the entire world witnessed the disastrous effect of such hatred culminating in mass destruction of lives and properties. By propagating hatred, people will only be adding fuel to the already burning fire in a world where violence and hatred abound.

The Bible makes it clear to us in Gen 1:26-27; that all humans are equal in the sight of God and we are made in the image of God, regardless of nationality, race or ethnicity. The scripture does not say that any one was made superior or inferior to anyone. Nevertheless, this has not prevented most people from accepting racist beliefs or ways.

[22] September 11, 2001: https://en.wikipedia.org/wiki/September_11_attacks

There seem to be a dominance of racist behavior and division across many societies and communities regardless of religion, ethnicity or race. Therefore, one can accurately conclude that because one is a Christians does not necessarily make such person less likely to imbibe racist beliefs than others.

Yet the bible continues to give us spiritual guidance on how we should relate with others. This tells us that any person who is willing can act rightly based on the Holy Word of God, so as to remove every bigotry of racism and division in their lives.

Racism has led to the destruction of lives on a wider scale. This can be seen during the slave trade where over 600 million Africans lost their lives en-route to the new world. Not to mention the destruction of over six million Jews by the Adolf Hitler led army. There are a lot of examples throughout history which supports this fact. Division and hatred manifested in diverse forms has not done us any good rather it has done more harm and will continue in this path unless we make a collective turnaround from our thoughts, actions and inactions which are selective, partial and divisive. Racial hatred, division, and destruction are weapons of mass destruction for a community and our world at large. Only peace, love and unity can counter these weapons and bring about perfect harmony.

Many of us look forward to a day when the entire world will come together in peace. This may never come to fruition and it may look like it will never happen any time soon but we must put our hands together to make it a reality in our own time. We must create a secure and safe environment for our children and generations yet unborn.

II.

Ignorance and Fear:

I sometimes find it difficult to understand how people today deliberately refuse to look at what is actually happening in the world around them; believing the lies and distortions that false leaders tell them. With a straight face such individuals as our civic leaders, economists, politicians, religious leaders, and media figures tell us that black is white, war is peace, lies are truths, joblessness is economic recovery, ignorance is intelligence, and hate is love.

If there is ever going to be an awakening or change in our society, it needs to begin now. Two of the most destructive factors to any society are the effects of ignorance and fear.

They harm us more than we can harm ourselves. Because of ignorance and fear; poverty, prejudice, and AIDS has been allowed to hound and kill our communities like a serial killer. Because of ignorance and fear war, hatred, social, and economic injustices are destroying the fabric of this nation at a rapid rate.

The prophet Hosea prophesied during a dark and gloomy era of Israel's history, the period of the Northern Kingdom's decline and fall in the 8th century BCE (before common era). The ignorance and fear of the people was rampant, having turned away from God in order to serve the calves of Jeroboam and Baal, a Canaanite god of fertility. Their conduct was the very opposite to that which God desired and demanded. The picture painted here was truly that of a nation in decay and a people spiritually lost.

Too often we have shifted the blame to the system being against us, and all types of other injustices. Though there are many social injustices, a lot of our current circumstances rest with us. In order for us to be able to overcome the issues that are there, we must first admit to it and take responsibility to our contribution to the degradation and breakdown of our communities and lives, and then take appropriate action of change to correct them.

The Time has come for us to realize that we deserve something better for ourselves and for our children. It's time for us to change and overcome our ignorance and fears. For in St. Timothy 1:7 it says "For God has not given us the spirit of fear; but of power, and love, and of a sound mind.

We must realize that God is not ignorant nor fearful but wise and bigger than any of our fears. Hopelessness; God is bigger. Broken and despair; God is bigger. Loneliness; God is bigger. Terrorist Attacks; God is Bigger. Economic downscale; God is bigger. Sickness; God is bigger. Social injustices; God is bigger. Discrimination; God is bigger. God has more power, more resources, and more intelligence than anything this world could ever offer.

We must learn to trust Him to deal with the unknown things we cannot see. No matter what happens, God will always be there.

The solution to ignorance and fear is simply trust; trust that is put in no one else but God. When your trust is solely in Him, peace of mind is your reward ignorance and fear flies right out the window. Trusting in God means that you recognize His authority and power over everything that may happen on earth and to you. When you trust in

God, you put your faith in Him, instead of in money, people, and government, and things. Those things will all fail one day, but God never will. Trusting God doesn't mean you'll never have fear in life, but it does mean that you can always look to Him for comfort, hope, strength, and wisdom. It also means that you don't have to worry, because God will always have your back.

Chapter 14

Put Away The Sword

In order to rise above human conflict caused by racial hostility, one must employ a strong character, tempered with endurance and tolerance, along with compassion and a desire to get closer to ones fellowman. Only then can one live more harmoniously with others. This is why the avoidance of violence, the promotion of peace, the resolution of conflicts by non-violent means, should be the subject of major concern to all world leaders, religious leaders, and all people of goodwill throughout the world. The swords, guns, and the bombs comes out, and people are stabbed, shot, electrocuted, gassed, annihilated, and slaughtered. We strike with the sword and so much more. We cut off an ear and so much more. We destroy entire countries and exterminate hundreds of thousands of people in a flicker of an eye. In fact, we are willing to risk the destruction of our entire planet for the sake of being the controlling factor. We strike back with violence to protect ourselves. We carry on because of the ever-present, ever-trusty, ever-faithful sword.

At this climactic point in the story as recorded in St. Matthew 26:52, as the soldiers put their hands on Jesus, arrest Him in the Garden of Gethsemane, and take Him away. Peter drew a sword and cut off the ear of Malchus, a slave of the high priest. When the sword was actually used, Jesus rebuked Peter, healed the wounded man, and said, "Put your sword back into its sheath, Jesus turns to His disciples for the final time. As He is dragged away by the authorities, He tells His community once again to reject violence, "for all who take the sword will perish by the sword."

The word "peace" was often on Jesus lips. Jesus not only followed a course of nonviolence and nonresistance He commanded His disciples and us today to do likewise. Those who take up the sword shall perish by the sword. Violence begets violence.

Killing begets killing. Nukes beget more nukes. Death begets death. Jesus stands for peace and not war. He will not yield to the way of violence and nor should we. Although Jesus knew that He would perish on Calvary's cross of violence, yet He placed His hope in the God of life and waited that third day for His resurrection from the grave.

The followers of Jesus are prohibited from drawing the sword. We are encouraged to love our enemies. As followers of Jesus we are to suffer violence rather than inflict it upon others. We should reject every form of violence, from nuclear capability, chemical or biological warfare, to handguns and assault weapons, to any form of dehumanization that causes harm or the life of a human being. We should renounce war and violence, and embrace the gospel of nonviolence. We should not only put away any swords we have but also encourage others to do the same. The unarmed Christ disarms us. Christ's community, the Church, is a community of nonviolence.

Jesus went beyond the condemnation of murder to condemn anger and contempt. He went beyond limited revenge "an eye for an eye and a tooth for a tooth" to unlimited forgiveness, "Not seven times, but, I tell you, seventy times seven. Do not judge or condemn your enemies, He says in St. Matthew 7:1 rather, love your enemies, do good to those who hate you, bless those who curse you, pray for those who abuse you.

When we turn, however, to the life of Jesus' dealing with His enemies, or His Sermon on the Mount, or to His warning to His nation regarding the Roman occupation, the uncertainty becomes inescapable. It is this side that has given the church an uneasy conscience regarding war and peace. Actions speak louder than words, so we shall start with Jesus' own actions in face of the hostility and persecution that confronted Him personally. Jesus' attitude toward revenge, when He was rejected and turned away from a Samaritan village, His disciples said, "Lord, do you want us to command fire to come down from heaven and consume them?" Jesus turned and rebuked them, and they went on to another village. It was not about revenge, or conflict rather peace," and the willingness to suffer pain. In situations like this even death transform the situation to one in which real peace becomes possible. The commands to follow Jesus' example are also promises to share His glory as "children of God."

The disciples were unable to comprehend Jesus' way of nonviolence. Over and over, Jesus instructs them to love their enemies and to lay down their lives for one another, thus preparing them for confrontation with the ruling forces and the inevitable outcome. But the disciples never understood Jesus' message. They heard His Sermon on the Mount, and they celebrated the Passover meal with Him. But they kept asking, "Lord, shall we strike with a sword?"

If we will obey the last words of Jesus, then we will not, like Judas, side with the enemy and employ their means of violence. We will instead suffer what Christ endured and take up our cross right alongside of Him. Jesus, the Son of God, stood for life and peace not war. He will not succumb to the way of violence, nor should we, as He said put away your sword and this is what we should do and accept peace over all for the welling being of all mankind!!

Chapter 15

Broken Promises:

40 Acres and A Mule

Have you heard the deep story behind the phrase "40 acres and a mule" a promise to former African slaves in America? It's a staple in black history. This pledge, according to history, was the first out-and-out attempt to provide a form of reparations to newly freed slaves, a promise rather radical for its time and implications. It is a promise of methodical redistribution of confiscated land and abandoned rice fields along the river bordering Charleston in the South, some 400,000 acres. It was a promise backed by the Freedmen's Bureau, which will allow free African-Americans to resettle as a colony to avoid already existed racism and prejudice in 1865.

However, less than one year after General William T. Sherman's order, President Abraham

Lincoln[23] was assassinated, and new President Andrew Johnson [24]interceded and requested that most by far of the confiscated land be given back to its previous proprietors. These lands included the greater part of an area that the freedmen had settled. The Federal government seized a vast number of black landholders. In South Carolina and Georgia, a few blacks tried to fight back, keeping away former owners with their guns. Government troops once in a while expelled these African-Americans by force. At last, somewhere in the range of 2,000 blacks retained land they had won and worked after the war.

Different provisions existed for the Blacks to get land, but they were inadequate. Under the Southern Homestead Act, prices were too high for previous slaves with no capital. The creation and implementation of Black Codes and year-long contracts to bind labor additionally made land acquisition nearly impossible. The Federal

---

[23]President Abraham Lincoln: http://www.biography.com/people/abraham-lincoln-9382540
[24]Andrew Johnson: https://en.wikipedia.org/wiki/Andrew_Johnson

government's retreat from its proposed land redistribution was not just a failure that developed a feeling of being double-crossed it was a missed opportunity for economic reform that may have permitted Southern African-Americans to consolidate and make political gains amid the early years of Reconstruction.

The failure to fulfill the '40 acres and a mule' promise had an enormous impact on African-Americans and the South as a whole. These African Americans fell into the share-cropping system; a system introduced by the ex-slave masters. This system was used by the white planters and merchants who were legislators; this was done to keep total control over the blacks.

Although they were legally free men, these men had to rely on the same people who had enslaved them for 246 years[25], for the basic needs of life to survive: shelter, food, clothing, farmland and farming supplies. After each passing year, they grew deeper and deeper in debt, binding them

---

[25] https://en.wikipedia.org/wiki/Slavery_in_the_United_States

further into a life of servitude. This system was another form of slavery.

So how have African-Americans faired without the "40 acres and a mule" promise?

Why still clamor for reparations? Here are a few accounts to give you a clue. Since 1619 when slavery became legal, White Americans have been amassing wealth from the lives of African-Americans. At the time of the Civil War, an average total of 4 million African-Americans were enslaved; about 13% of America's total population.

After the civil war, institutional injustices were used to rob what was left of them, ensuring that African-Americans did not build wealth for themselves to pass on like the rest of Americans. This act was the premise on which the U.S. economy, we have today is built.

It was slavery that launched modern capitalism and transformed the U.S. into the wealthiest country in the world. It was cotton that made New York City into a financial and commercial center. In the 19th century, slave-harvested cotton dominated the international market leading to the U.S. contributing more than 70% cotton used in the British textile industry and many other parts of Europe.

Meanwhile, emancipation did not bring economic freedom to former slaves. The American nation paid reparations to slaveholders - not to the slaves. President Andrew Johnson overturned the proposed "40 acres and a mule" promise, aimed to redistribute about 400,000 acres of land to newly freed black families to resettle, away from racism and prejudice. Incidentally, vagrancy laws allowed police to sweep up black men and rent them out as convict labor, making the Southern prison population predominantly black.

On the other hand, discriminatory business policies kept white Americans economically ahead and prevented African-Americans from receiving help other citizens receive. Black Codes were enacted to hinder African-Americans from owning their enterprises and houses. Most Southern merchants used bad credit to impede blacks from building wealth; they were lending blacks credit at 44%-74% in Georgia against a 7% lending rate in New York City.

What more, social safety programs have always missed African-Americans, Social security initially excluded domestic and agricultural workers - mostly blacks, especially in the South. Racist policies contributed immensely to the decline of black farmers. According to a survey in 1982, only 1.5% of farmers were blacks and the USDA's Civil Rights Office that investigated loan program discrimination complaints - was closed down. And many more unjust acts were perpetrated against blacks...

So what is the result? African-Americans have not been able to get a foothold in the American economy. African-Americans barely have a hold of the nation's wealth therefore have little to pass down to future generations. Experts say that up to 80% of lifetime wealth accumulation depends on intergenerational transfers. Since 1865, the national wealth owned by African-Americans has not grown more than 1%, and the income gap between the whites and the blacks has not budged since 1970. According to historians, fulfilling the "40 acres and a mule" promise today would free African-Americans to economically decide their future and have a black colony as large as Texas with wealth in the area of $6.4 trillion, making African-Americans self-sufficient and capable of providing for future generations.

Chapter 16
How Long Must We Keep Marching?

America is a wonderful nation with unlimited freedoms and opportunities. Yet, a nation that still fails to address the race issue which has plagued this nation for decades. The world looks to this nation for guidance and direction, but when a certain group of people in this nation gets into their minds that the hands of time needs to go backward to a time when it was common for one race of people to enslave, dehumanize, mistreat, to deny the basic human rights of another, and even murder them because of the color of their skin. They have not learned how wonderful it is when people of different races can come together for the common good of all of mankind.

During the era of Dr. Martin Luther King Jr. African-Americans and people of other races marched in the streets, highways, and byways for justice, fair treatment under the law, job opportunities, and to be counted as human beings. More than 40 years after the death of Dr. King, we are still marching against racism, segregation, demanding justice, fair treatment and jobs; we are still demanding the same things that Dr. King and other leaders fought and died for during their time.

In protest of the brutal deaths of Travyon Martin, Michael Brown, Eric Garner, Aiyana Mo'Nay Stanley Jones, Walter Scott, Tamir Rice, Renisha Mcbride, Sandra Bland and others whom had perished at the hands of the corrupt. People from all ages, walks of life, ethnic groups took to the streets, the airwaves, and social media demanding justice. Some are still seeking justice to this day, despite the fact that after months and years have passed since the deaths of these people. Although the marching and demonstrations may have ceased but the call for justice continues for these victims.

The big question remains, when will the marching and demonstrations end and justice and fair treatment be achieved? When will the picket signs come down?

I feel that not until the hearts and minds of people are changed where love, peace, and unity are portrayed in our society. Not until real change is achieved across this nation and true brotherhood is achieved, will the marching end.

Jesus said in the scripture that "the poor you will always have with you". The same goes for racism: it will always be with us. So then, what should be done about it? There are many strategies to adopt in fighting racism: you may protest, march, beg or complain to the government of the day. Some of these strategies have worked in the past. However, one of the most effective weapons to fight racism today is excellence. It will bulldoze more racial barriers than all the protesting and complaining in the world.

Although considerable progress has been made in tackling racism, it still leaves much to be desired. However, if one has the ability for critical thinking, it will be a lot difficult for such a person to be a racist.

No matter how someone may look in appearance, they are still human beings, and it means that they are a part of the human race. Bearing this in mind, the human heart will only know love and would not judge.

Just like the creatures of the deep, racism is very much alive. You may not see it before you but it is very real and active. It may not be as severe as it was in the past; however, the existing systems in place still encourage discrimination towards blacks and people of other races. We have all tried it: peaceful protesting, rioting, getting laws changed and taking down flags, all in a bid to solve this age old problem.

At times the problem might be that it is not recognized as a problem in the first place. Could it be true that up till this point, many Americans do not consider racism as one of the issues that need urgent attention in today's society? President

Obama was on to something when he said we could end racism if we wanted to. If we want to rise above it, everyone will have to make a little extra effort. This highlights the fact that society does not really consider racism to be a problem. And that's disappointing to know that people still haven't woke up to the concept that we are all human beings and we are all made of the same stuff and occupy this one planet and it would be beneficial for us to live in peace, unity, harmony and love.

Perhaps it may not be possible to end racism in this generation, but to reach a decision that racism cannot end in this generation or in the near future will hinder it from ever coming to an end.

So to put an end to racism we must understand that racism has been in existence right from the inception of time and has not come to an end yet. Because we consider the problem of racism as too huge to eliminate or solve, we shy away from fighting it with the hope that future generations will fight this fight. We need to take a stand now and speak out against the issues of racism and discrimination.

How about each one making the subject of racism a part of our daily conversation and when our conversation hits a dead end, we keep pushing until we find a way through, until other people become interested in the same conversation and they begin to discuss racial discrimination with one another. And during that conversation someone ask the question, what can we do to bring an end to this age old program that has plague our society? We are not perfect in anyway but we should strive to unify ourselves with one another. Now I ask you, what are you doing to end racism?

Chapter 17

We The People

The first three words of the United States Constitution Preamble [26]reads "We the People". It does not say "We The Black People", "We The White People", "We The Red People", "We The Brown People" or We The Yellow People but "We The People" who come together to form a most perfect union, establish justice, insure domestic tranquility, provide for the common defense, promote the general welfare, and secure the blessings of liberty to ourselves and our posterity, do ordain and establish the constitution for the United States of America.

These words are powerful and speak volume to a people that has been long forgotten and plagued by racism, discrimination, segregation, injustice, violence, inequality, and murder. How

---

[26]The United States Constitution: http://www.constitution.org

can we make these words inclusive that they mean the same for all people, not just some but for all? "We The People" is a unified inclusive statement to all people.

There is no doubt that we need to discover a healthy solution to discrimination in whatever form it presents itself. It is also imperative that we understand the nature of racism and disharmony. Together we can end intolerance; and our quest to end racial discrimination cannot be won when people harbor thoughts that make them manifest racist tendencies.

The ability to understand and accept that we are all equal and should be united regardless of race is prerequisite for us to live in peace and harmony.

Race-based prejudice and disharmony are present today as they were in time past. Even with more stringent state and federal laws, racial discrimination continues to increase. Most individuals regardless of race, nationality or ethnicity whom would not ordinarily be seen as racist propagate racism through their behaviors, speech and thoughts.

The challenge we face today is not that people have stopped talking about race, but have begun using coded color-blind terms such as "criminals," "drug dealers," "thugs," "gangsters," "urban underclass," "inner cities," "terrorists," "hijackers," "suicide bombers," "Islamic fundamentalists," "welfare queens," "crack mothers," "hyperfertile mothers," "illegal aliens," "gangs," "drug cartels," and "taxpayer burdens" have become the coded terms used by society to talk about race, gender, sexuality, and nationality.

On the surface many people champion the crusade against racism and pretend to tolerate people of other race, but in reality they are not being honest about their true opinions which they harbor in their minds. Why is it that some people act in a racist manner even when they claim to take a stand against racism?

Jesus says in St. Matthew 12:34 "Out of the abundance of the heart, the mouth speaketh." This means that you cannot claim that you do not have racist intent or harbor racist motives or thoughts and yet you cast racist insults and make racist remarks concerning people of other races. This is indeed the truth because a racist mind will empty its thoughts in the form of actions, behavior, and words. Yet, many people still maintain that their racist remark against others does not in any way imply that they have racist intentions.

Racism destroys unity and oneness: the foundation on which the constitution of the United States stands. Both the mind of the individual on the receiving end and the person who perpetrates racism is adversely affected by this societal ill. Everyone regardless of nationality, ethnicity or race should through the guidance of God's spirit search their hearts for areas where racial bias or prejudice may hold sway.

Racism is a belief system which is based on ignorance, distorted perversion and hatred. Many have come to accept that we exist in a pluralistic society and we appreciate diverse cultures. But there are still an appreciable number of people who would not accept that capacities of human beings are not determined by what race they belong to.

Racial discrimination is an issue that is difficult to tackle and in order to form a society free of racist behavior which the constitution of the United States stands for we must exploit the tool of education. We must teach our children tolerance towards race, color, religion and sexual orientation, if we do not want them to grow up in a world full of hatred. We must expose discrimination and injustice for what they truly are, a cancer on our society.

We must create an enabling environment for our children to relate with people of different races. Your children should learn to accept people of other races; teach them that there is no room for segregation. Bear in mind that children are influenced by their environment in which they live.

Racism is not something that will go away just like that, and the earlier we join forces together to tackle it, the sooner we will arrive at a solution.

Racism and all forms of discrimination has a history which cannot be erased, but we can see ahead with hope in our minds while we try to change how people see those of different ethnic and racial origin.

X-ray your own opinions and attitudes towards individuals of a different racial origin. Before labeling people, think about how your actions are affecting the world.

It will be hypocritical if we do not get to purify ourselves of the same faults that we point out in other people. Therefore, the first step in combating discrimination and prejudices in all of its forms is to examine ourselves. Ask God to help you identify all the aspects of your life where you may have inadvertently aided the propagation of discrimination and disunity and pray for Him to change you completely and renew a right spirit within you.

Chapter 18

The Beloved Community

The history of the beloved community can be traced to the early days of the 20th century. This perfect community was first visualized by the Philosopher and Theologian Josiah Royce [27]who was the founder of Fellowship of Reconciliation. This term was made popular by the late Dr. Martin Luther King, Jr.[28] through his ability to empower the world with a much deeper meaning thus capturing the minds and imaginations of the people all over the world. To Dr. King, there shouldn't be any sort of confusion or comparison of the beloved community with any unrealistic goal displaying harmony. But rather, a realistic community which has set an achievable and well-structured goal that can only be attained by a certain group and caliber

---

[27]Josiah Royce: https://en.wikipedia.org/wiki/Josiah_Royce
[28] Dr. Martin Luther King, Jr.: The Beloved Community,
http://www.thekingcenter.org

of people, people who have love and determination in their hearts; people who are trained and committed in the way of philosophy and non-violence strategies of achieving goals.

The beloved community is not a locally oriented dream but a global vision in which all people of all ethnic background, religion, and creed can live happily and share in the wealth this world of ours has to offer. In this wonderful and beloved community, hunger, poverty and homelessness will be prohibited nor tolerated, because it would never be allowed by the international standards of human decency. Racism and all forms of hatred will only be read in history books, because they would have been replaced by love and the spirit of brotherhood. In the beloved community, disagreements and disputes will be resolved amicably in a non-conflict manner instead of the normal violent approach. Love will triumph over fear and trust over hatred. War and military conflict will be replaced with peace and justice. The idea of Dr. King's beloved community was not completely emphasizing on a community absent of interpersonal, organization or international conflict because he believed that human being are naturally programmed to disagree and see things differently thus giving room for some forms of indifferences which could results into conflicts. But he believed that resolving conflicts shouldn't be through the hard way of violence but a resolution of peaceful, mutual and nonviolence agreement. And every occurring conflict in the beloved community should be ended with true reconciliation and an enhanced spirit of friendship and togetherness.

Across the U.S. and parts of the world, every third Monday in January is a day dedicated to honoring and celebrating the life of Dr. Martin Luther king, Jr. to honor his passion, impact and role towards a non-violent peaceful change in our world. One of his statement was "I want to challenge each of us to create this dream in our own lives", the dream of The Beloved Community. An illustrative representation of the beloved community can be related to two-fold dream which are the balancing of racial equality and Compassion and Economic Justice for everyone. Without these two, peace and economic justice cannot happen. If the world is absent of compassion and economic justice, the poor will always get poorer, discrimination will never leave our society, and our proclaimed change would only be a illusion yet unleashed, just like it is happening in some of our countries.

This kind of justice which denotes liberty for all shouldn't end here, it should extend to every area of our life, we would be free to marry anyone of our choice irrespective of their race, ethnic group, religion even sexual orientation. In a liberty society, women will be treated equally with their reproductive choices. Liberty and justice preaches that we don't have to take prisoners through the rigorous process of torture, we don't need to hold them endlessly without a trial, we don't have to terrorize them with the Nazi tactics and deceive ourselves as someone who appreciates freedom and human rights. "There are unjust men, as there are unjust laws."

Compassion for others is great, but it is not enough, it is important to couple compassion with willingness and the ability to stand for what is good, just and right. The beloved community won't just sit back and relent in its comfort zone, but instead will allow us to stand and offer an helping hand to those outside of our comfort zone who are suffering from injustice due to the lack of compassion. This wonderful community is not a one-sided or nationally focused living pattern but a human based dynamic way of life. As individuals, we must endeavor to posse both sides of this equation to be able to emulate the realistic and beneficial beliefs of Dr. King. We are one and it is important for us to live as thus. Many of our religious organization go well with this belief and we appreciate this. Regardless of your spiritual pursuits, I urge you to acknowledge and instill compassion and economic justice into every thought and action of your life as a whole.

The beloved community does not discriminate against people of other various spiritual beliefs, but instead embraces and relates with them. "It's easy to extend love to our friends. The challenge is to do so to our enemies. That's the real test of our spirituality and our humanity."

To carry out the strategy of the beloved community, we must explore all educational opportunities available that will enhance our world. Although the doors of opportunity may not always be open to everyone, there are yet other ways to achieve what you want to achieve, have what you want to have, and be what you want to be. How you live, how poor you are, and where you live are immaterial. The ability to live in peace and love with your fellowman is possible and it lies within each of us. This is possible so long as you have the desire to change your world around you.

Despite the fact that the doors of opportunity are not available to everybody, one thing that we all have is time. Every one of us has the same number of hours in a day. It is your choice what you do with your time. You can either use them in productive ventures or use them carelessly. Whiling away useful time engaging in the pleasures of life can only give you few hours of satisfaction but engaging in productive ventures will give you gratifications in the long run.

In order to achieve "The Beloved Community" we must look up and within ourselves as we look with hope towards a better tomorrow. In our quest to make the beloved community an object of realism, we should find ways to go beyond our comfort zone. First lets respect and practice being human, and understand the voice behind every joy and sorrows of our fellow travelers in this journey of life.

In conclusion, any forms of discrimination will only bring nothing but setbacks to the progress already made as human beings and also to the world, let's put aside our differences and come together in love. For love is the answer that will solve the many conflicts in our world and bring all people from all races and walks of life together in perfect harmony and unity. For no one should be an island isolated from the storms of life. If The Beloved Community is to become a reality, real change must take place in the hearts and mind of all people, as this will be the foundation and the beginning for the Beloved Community to be revealed to our world.

A Prayer for Unity

Heavenly Father,

You hold us in Your hands for we are all Your Children made in Your image and for that we thank You.

Father, help us to accept our differences. Help us to use our diversity to share with each other, for the richness of our many cultures, languages and backgrounds enriches our world making it a better place for all to live.

Father, help us to dissolve the many man-made barriers caused by the evil of racism as we unite to work for a just world in which none are hated, discriminated against, isolated, abandoned, mistreated, or murdered on the basis of their race, creed, religion, sex, or any other man-made barriers, as all of us are valued for their true humanity.

Father, help us to embrace each other and the true meaning of sisterhood and brotherhood and allow us to promote peace, harmony, unity, and love as we strive for that beloved community.

Father, we ask all of this in the name of Our Lord and Savior Jesus Christ, who saw beyond all human divisions, human fragilities, and reached out to the good within each of us, this we ask in Jesus Name, Amen.

About the Author:
Dr. Christopher D. Handy, PhD
Author/Lecturer/Teacher/Minister

o Having a dream to re-build decaying communities and lives by making the world a better place for all of humanity to live in peace and harmony. The Rev. Dr. Christopher D. Handy strives to raise the conscience of people everywhere to make a difference. His meager beginnings in a small rural town in Monroe, Louisiana and his childhood in a housing project greatly contributed to his mission to enlighten, inform, educate, and motivate people to better themselves, their communities, and the world around them.

o Dr. Handy has written many books, articles for various newspapers and magazines. He has organized marches to combat violence, injustices, and poverty, and while in school in

Michigan he ministered on the 'bad' streets of Detroit and other cities. He continues to uphold justice and freedom by sharing his experiences with audiences everywhere. His first book "The Scars of Racism" has made a stunning and positive impact on people of all races.

o In 1999, Dr. Handy founded a Non-denomination Christian Community Church Ministry called The New Testament Bible Church and a non-profit organization called I.C.A.N (Innovative Community Action Network); Dr. Handy main focus is the future of our younger generation and the out casts of our society. In effort to prepare all young boys and men for the realization of being a man in today's society, he has developed a program called "Christian Manhood Training Program" (CMTP), which is a rites of passage program which deals with many of today's tough issues such as developing a relationship with God, treatment of women, responsibility of being a Father, learning to love and not Kill, the importance of an education, handling racism, and the dangers of drugs and alcohol abuse.

o Dr. Handy is currently the CEO/President/Executive Director of Innovative Community Action Network (I.C.A.N.). His focus is working with at-risk and troubled youths, the poor and needy, the disenfranchised, and those without hope within the community by helping them to believe in themselves and encouraging them to strive for success. He was honored in 2002 with an Honorary Doctorate of Humanities Degree from The Institute of Christian Works for his work with his Mentoring Program for at-risk and troubled youths. Dr. Handy is also a certified prison fellowship counselor, who has spoken to numerous inmates of all ages on how to survive on the inside, thus, preparing them for their release into society. Dr. Handy is a Licensed and Certified Counselor/Certified Life skills Coach and Trainer/Adult Organizational Development Specialist. Dr. Handy is a Certified Private Postsecondary Educator in Christian Education. Dr. Handy is the President/Chancellor/Founder of The New Testament Bible Church Biblical Institute. He serves as Professor of Theology and Practice of Ethics and Ministry. In April 2011, Dr. Handy was appointed **Bishop of the Louisiana Conference** from Fellowship of Christ International; his appointment was accredited to his many years of dedicated service to God, service to humanity, and ministry. His district covers the entire state of Louisiana.

o His educational background includes studies in Business Administration from Louisiana Business College, a Bachelor's Degree in

Religious Education, and a Bachelor's Degree in Theology, a Master's of Divinity Degree, and a Doctorate of Theology Degree from Andersonville Baptist Seminary in Camilla, Ga. He has a Ph. D. in Philosophy in Counseling from the Institute of Christian Works in Columbia; SC. Dr. Handy is the Father of three children and definitely believes the family is the foundation of any society. Dr. Handy has received many citations and special recognition awards from many states and civic organizations across the US.

Other Books by Dr. Handy

- o The Scars of Racism

- o Readings For The Soul

- o A Christian Guide To A New You

- o Love Letters To My Future Bride and Wife To Be

- o Help Lord, My Life Hurts

- o What Does It Means To Be A Christian?

- o Saving Our Children

Please address your correspondence to:

Dr. Christopher D. Handy, PhD

P.O. Box 7514

Monroe, Louisiana 71211

E-mail Address: drcdhandy@gmail.com

http://www.revchristopherhandy.com